THE LIFE AND CRIMES OF
CONOR McGREGOR

CHAOS IS A FRIEND OF MINE

THE LIFE AND CRIMES OF
CONOR McGREGOR

EWAN MACKENNA

deCoubertin
B O O K S

First published by deCoubertin Books Ltd in 2019.

First Edition

deCoubertin Books, 46b Jamaica Street, Baltic Triangle, Liverpool, L1 0AF.
www.decoubertin.co.uk

ISBN: 978-1-909245-90-7

A CIP catalogue record for this book is available from the British Library.

Cover design and Typeset by Thomas Regan | Milkyone Creative.

Printed and bound by Ashford Print.

Para Erika e Putchi.

Obrigado por sua tolerância e paciência, por seu amor e apoio.

ABOUT THE AUTHOR

Born in Ireland, Ewan MacKenna is an award-winning journalist and author. He first interviewed Conor McGregor in 2013 after his maiden UFC victory, and has followed his career closely ever since, including covering his fight with Khabib Nuragomedov at UFC 229 in Las Vegas in 2018. A former Irish Sportswriter of the Year, he is a columnist with the *Irish Independent* and has also contributed internationally to *The New York Times*, *Bleacher Report*, *ESPN* and the *Independent*. He splits his time between Portugal, Brazil and Ireland.

CONTENTS

FOREWORD

BY WRIGHT THOMPSON

I INTERVIEWED CONOR MCGREGOR ONCE, FOR MAYBE fifteen minutes, and then he drove out into the Las Vegas desert in a bright green Lamborghini. I liked him in that short time, found him confident, humble and, if this makes sense, scared just behind the bravado. Not scared of any man, mind you. In that regard, he exuded a fearlessness I envied. He seemed scared in the way that all newly successful fighters are scared: that his new life might be a mirage, that it might turn into dust like the endless sands surrounding the neon of his temporary American home, that he might end up back where he began: with nothing, and even worse, a nobody.

While I was in Nevada for that McGregor interview, I drove my car to a cemetery just behind the international airport, where a private jet brings Conor into town. He flew directly over it. After parking, and searching pictures and videos on the internet to triangulate landmarks and trees, I finally found the grave of Sonny Liston. He's buried beneath fake flowers. His epitaph says, simply, 'A man.' He conquered the world and died broke, of a drug overdose that some people still believe was a mafia hit. Famously he said something that ended up prophetically applying to him and might apply to everyone who tries to change their lives with their fists, including Conor McGregor: 'Some day, they're gonna write a blues song just for fighters. It'll be for slow guitar, soft trumpet, and a bell.'

* * *

TO FIND AN IRISH FIGHTER AS CULTURALLY

important as McGregor, you've got to go back a long way. You know this history by heart but forgive me a little explanation, for the sake of a clean narrative and for any American readers who have picked up this book. Irish history was broken in the 1840s and 1850s when the island shed its poorest working-class citizens during the potato famine. A million died and a million left. The people who left took their traditions to a new world, prizefighting among them. It's no coincidence that the 500-year-old Donnybrook Fair, which featured heavy drinking and cartoonish violence and gave the modern world a new word for a brawling riot, ended in 1855, just after the famine took away the people who loved it most. Those people landed in the United States, and what should have been an Irish boxing tradition became American.

John L. Sullivan, the last great bareknuckle fighter, and James J. Corbett, the first great gloved fighter, were both the sons of men who landed in the U.S. in the early 1850s. Before the final world title fight ever fought with bare knuckles, in 1889, Sullivan was interviewed for a magazine by Nellie Bly.

'Do you like prizefighting?' she asked.

'I don't,' he said.

'Why?'

'I am getting old,' he said. 'I have made plenty of money in my day, but I have been a fool and today I have nothing. It came easy and went easy. I have provided well for my father and mother.'

'How much money have you made?'

'I have made $500,000 or $600,000 in boxing,' he said, which in today's dollars would be $14,947,653.

The closest an Irish fighter from the past comes to approaching the nationalist fervour hung round McGregor's shoulders was a man named Dan Donnelly. He beat two English champions and carried the banner for Irish pride at a time when the English had defeated Napoleon and Waterloo and took joy in keeping a boot on Irish pride and identity. He fought his two most famous fights in a little green valley an hour outside Dublin, in front of 20,000 fans – the same number that can fit in Las Vegas's T-Mobile arena. The rules of the day allowed wrestling and butting – much closer to McGregor's style than Mayweather's. After his second and most famous victory, he walked away from the ring and up and over a hill into the fields. Rabid fans followed and dug up grass and dirt from his footsteps to take home a souvenir. A parade led him back into Dublin, and his mother walked at the front, one of her breasts exposed as she shouted for people to look upon the tit that suckled him.

That really happened. He was a national treasure.

He grew up in the south inner city, less than ten blocks from the Holiday Inn where the Drimnagh-Crumlin feud began; the feud in his day, every bit as violent and bloody as anything in a present-day Dublin tabloid, pitted the Liberty Boys, who were tailors and weavers from the south side, against the Ormond Boys, who were butchers from north of the river. Donnelly managed a bar near the river, almost exactly on the spot where a popular music club named Mulligan's is located today, which is a favourite of Jamie Kavanagh the boxer. His second bar is still open, under a new name, at the end of where Crumlin Road changes names and leads into the city centre. In all, he drank away three pubs and died broke in his fourth, the last one on the north side, a half block from where the Irish Boxing Union is now headquartered. He was just 32 when he died. 'I have been given so much,' he said to his wife on his death bed, 'and I have done so little.'

He was buried in a pauper's cemetery. Grave robbers stole his body to sell to medical students, a popular industry at the time, and the city fell into outrage. The body was returned, minus his famous right arm, which someone removed and kept. Today, if you take a quiet road past the horse farms and at least one heavy bag hanging outside a farmer's house, there is a faded and weathered stone marker, denoting the spot where Dan Donnelly once became the champion of the world. The hollow is quiet, with gorse now covering the hillsides, smelling green and fresh. His footsteps remain in the ground, 48 of them, climbing up to a fence with a single strand of barbed wire. Back in a nearby village, there's a woman sitting at her kitchen table with some guests, overlooking her garden. She and her husband once owned a pub, which his father owned before them, and on the wall of that pub hung Dan Donnelly's arm, which made its way from the thieving doctor to Scotland to Belfast to the outskirts of Dublin.

She took it out and laid it on the white table next to a little vase of yellow flowers. It had been preserved in lead paint, almost mummified, and the ball socket is still visible, along with his fingernails. His hand was curled, with one finger extended, pointing at something. She took the arm to America a few times for exhibits, and it always rode in the cockpit of an Aer Lingus flight, courtesy of a friend who was a pilot. Then she carefully wraps up Donnelly's arm in cloth and puts it back in the box.

'It's older than New York,' she says.

* * *

A FEW YEARS AGO, ON THE EVE OF THE MAYWEATHER fight, my profile on McGregor ran and I found myself in a modern media storm: a segment of Dublin was angry at me for exaggerating the violence of Conor's past and his old neighbourhood, while Conor's team was angry at me for putting their lives at risk by writing about the gangland world he still moves around at home. He grew up surrounded by members of rival gangs whose feuds often spill onto the front pages of the tabloids. There'd even been a shooting at the weigh-in of a local boxing match. Gang bosses lurked around the fringes of Conor's circle and if it weren't for fighting, he very well could have ended up an enforcer.

A segment of what seemed like hipster Dublin was attacking the story for being fiction; they said I depicted a city they didn't recognize. One person said this story made them reconsider all my stories. Exhibit A seemed to hinge on a verb tense issue.

The original draft read: *Men older than 50 remember having to drop dates off at bus stops instead of walking them all the way home.*

The final draft read: *Men have had to drop dates off at bus stops instead of walking them all the way home.*

Those two sentences, which say the same thing, although the edited version says it more succinctly but less clearly, got referenced in all the blowback. An *Irish Times* columnist said she didn't know she 'should have been taking an armed escort whenever I had to cross the Liffey'.

So while one part of Dublin said I was full of shit, McGregor's camp asked for the story to be taken down. One member of his inner circle said the story put his family in danger.

I learned a few important lessons.

One, I clearly should have been much more clear in the writing, because the neighbourhood where Conor grew up, the ethos of which still lives in its sons and daughters, has been gentrified and, as many e-mails said, you can live an entire life there and never know there's a shadow world all around you. And if I'm being honest, the reaction strung, because the fact that people liked my stories in Ireland had always meant a lot to me, and I'd always felt a kinship with the place that got damaged in the fall out.

Two, related to that and this book, we all live in our own world. I spoke to people who grew up in the rough Crumlin for whom their home was a place to be reckoned with and ultimately escaped. I got emails from people for whom it's just another part of a sprawling modern global city.

Neither of those people could see each other.

And so Conor McGregor occupies his unique place in Irish public life, as a cypher – or a shibboleth even – a kind of Rosetta stone that translates how you feel about your home and your country and your future. The tabloids love him. The big dailies think he represents a cancer in Irish society. He's a hero in the council estates and a pariah in polite circles.

He is whatever people want him to be.

But…

* * *

BUT… WHATEVER SOMEONE THINKS ABOUT HIM, HE is the one suffering the pain and taking the risk – exchanging that pain and risk for a new life, a rebirth even – and to my American eye, that feels essentially Irish. One day on the banks of the Liffey before meeting McGregor's father at a local MMA event, I passed the

Famine Memorial and felt a heavy wave of ghosts. I'm from America, from a Scotch-Irish family, which means my people got on ships and headed into the unknown ocean hoping for a better life. I've always felt deeply at home in Ireland, whether at the bar at Grogan's or out in the trout stream countryside, because I think some of those memories and cultural DNA still remain somehow.

I also realise that the Ireland of my imagination bears little or no resemblance to the actual nation; my place is an empty desert, where all the people are gone, out in the world seeking. I love listening to the Pogues' 'Thousands are Sailing' when I'm in Ireland, because it hammers home to me that the birth of America is in many ways an act of Irish imagination, and that the Irish spirit and identity are so strong that they don't need things like nation-states to survive. To be Irish, from my distant view, is an act of imagination.

Conor McGregor is a lot of things. He is a champion and a successful businessman. He is a father, a devoted one from the looks of it. He is a son and a brother. He is also a violent man, in his workplace and out of it. He is accused of all manner of anti-social and criminal acts. But most of all, he is a self-invention – a creation of will and spirit and, most of all, imagination.

That's the man who comes to life on the pages of the book in your hand, and the nation that comes to life around him, where we learn something about ourselves as humans, and about Ireland as a place, from seeing McGregor move through the world and seeing his fellow citizens react to that movement. There are many stories on display in these pages, about Ireland, about violence, about modern civilization, but there is a central story running through all of them: What price is a man willing to pay for a new life and what does paying that price do to that man's ability to enjoy and protect his rebirth, and pass that on to his heirs?

* * *

EWAN AND I, ALONG WITH SO MANY OF OUR PEERS, are often called to write about fighters – both the stars and those who get pummelled by stars to pay their bills. Writing about modern fights automatically accesses all the men who've stepped into the ring or cage before him, so that Conor McGregor doesn't exist alone but as part of a continuum, one in a long line of people who wanted to literally fight their way to a better life, stripping life of metaphor and leaving only blood and pain behind. There's a clean line from McGregor to Mike Tyson to Dan Gable to Dan Donnelly. Boxing history exists as a warning.

I wrote once about the fifty men who faced Muhammad Ali.

One of them, Jimmy Robinson, had disappeared, and the story ended up being about the nature of existence – what does it mean to occupy this earth? – that chiselled through the one-hand-clapping idea that such proximity to one of the most famous humans ever must guarantee someone at least a measure of immortality. My story destroyed the notion of fame and history. In it, I found out what happened to the men who fought Ali, and discovered the price they paid for that meeting, for the life that brought them to that meeting, and in nearly every case it was more extreme than the terrible price Ali himself paid for his new life. I'd like to reprint that list of opponents here.

Tunney Hunsaker, Ali's first opponent, spent nine days in a coma after a bout.

Trevor Berbick, Ali's final opponent, was beat to death with a steel pipe.

Herb Siler went to prison for shooting his girlfriend.

Tony Esperti went to prison for a Mafia hit in a Miami Beach nightclub.

Alfredo Evangelista went to prison in Spain.

Alejandro Lavorante died from injuries sustained in the ring.

Sonny Banks did, too.

Jerry Quarry died broke, his mind scrambled from dementia.

Jimmy Ellis suffered from it, too.

Rudi Lubbers turned into a drunk and joined a carnival.

Buster Mathis blew up to 550 pounds and died of a heart attack at 52.

George Chuvalo lost three sons to heroin; his wife killed herself after the second son's death.

Oscar Bonavena was shot through the heart with a high-powered rifle outside a Reno whorehouse.

Cleveland Williams was killed in a hit-and-run.

Zora Folley died mysteriously in a motel swimming pool.

Sonny Liston died of a drug overdose in Las Vegas.

Liston is buried beneath fake flowers, underneath the airplanes that take people in and out of a city that offers a new life and often manages to deliver just that, only not the gilded, shiny one all those believers imagined as their planes came out of the clouds into the desert. I'm talking about gamblers who can't afford that all-in, about small town beauties who don't yet know how they'll pay their bills, and about generations of fighters for whom Las Vegas is a battleground, from Ali to McGregor. It's a desert, after all, no matter what lie the neon tells. Ozymandias is profound for a reason. The sand is unrelenting and undefeated.

Wright Thompson, October 2019

INTRODUCTION

IT'S 6 OCTOBER, 2019 – A YEAR ON FROM A NIGHT IN
Las Vegas where Conor McGregor had the years catch up with him in
the octagon. He was well beaten then and there, transforming from a
youthful hero with the world spread out before him like a dream and
on into an old man that talked the talk but could no longer walk. On
the canvas, after the hiding he took from the brilliant Khabib Nurmagomedov, there was further humiliation as members of his opponent's
team attacked him. Soon after his fans went on the rampage up and
down the city's famed strip into the early hours.

The walls had finally come tumbling down. Today I'm sitting
watching my one-year-old nephew Oscar run from one end of the
living room clasping a toy car, before running back again in a frenzy. It

gets me thinking about the swings and roundabouts that shape people. McGregor himself was once a small and innocent boy like this, waiting to be moulded by life as it opened out in front of him. It also gets me thinking that when this small and innocent boy before me is older and grows a curiosity about the past, how will I explain McGregor to him?

There haven't been too many like him in sport, and there certainly have been none like him in Irish sport. One moment people pointed at the guy who came from nothing, as if a path to follow for those on the breadline and as if some example of how hard work and belief can get you anywhere. The next moment they pointed at the guy who seemed to have thrown it all away and is now left with as much misery as money, not to mention those he's alleged to have inflicted untold and life-changing misery on. They cannot and should not be forgotten in this.

There have always been those who think they can become so big that they can merely step over the chasm. He's a great modern example of this being false and of pride coming before that fall.

We await to see what happens to him next. In MMA. And in life. On the one hand he's on Twitter talking about a return to the octagon and a homecoming via a Dublin fight, but no one believes him anymore. On the other hand we await to see where a criminal investigation, widely reported in the US media, goes.

McGregor always fascinated me since his major breakthrough in 2013, but not for the same reasons that drew the gazes and then the purchases of so many. To be a champion in UFC was all he ever wanted back then, but the byproduct of money and fame that came shackled to that have eaten away at a once likeable character. His old self no longer seems to exist, crushed by making it so big, with the latest video emerging involving McGregor appearing to punch an old man in a bar as he rejected his offer of a free whiskey. That's another one that the authorities will decide on soon.

So many that once cheered him on have already turned (and you can't blame them if what's claimed is in any way true).

For me, he's become a representation of the ills of society, but also a creation of those ills. A microcosm of the anger and rage that has seen politics swerve so far to the right. A mirror of the need and the greed in a society where your earnings matter far more than your morals ever could.

There's sport. But he has transcended it and became something far greater.

It was in 2016 that a call came through suggesting this book. The idea began as a biography but to go strictly down that route would be a waste, as to look at McGregor in isolation and solely in terms of his art and not in the context of the world around him, would be to miss so much.

Thus you won't find pages of MMA analysis around each of his triumphs and disasters in the octagon. You won't find an inventory of his cars and Rolex collection to wow those impressed by that nonsense.

You won't find the breasts-out, pants-down tales of women that claim to have slept with him in order to lazily hoist themselves into public consciousness.

If that's what you want, then this isn't for you.

Go away. Get out of here. Be gone.

It may seem a strange way to begin a book by trying to get rid of large swathes of potential buyers, but there's a division in the world we now live in. Between those lusting after the gossip, building up the hero, and then destroying that person for their own amusement, and those curious about the cause and effect of those forces. Between those who measure a football match in passing percentages and quarterbacks by SuperBowl rings, and those who are fascinated by people and where their journeys take them.

I've never cared for Conor McGregor's social media following or his net worth. However, I have cared for his tale and for his sanity, given what he's been thrust into. Others cheer his chaos. However, it's really tragedy.

Talking to the journalist Wright Thompson a while back, he mentioned how there's a complete lack of understanding around the effect that celebrity has on stars. It's true as, while this fame-laden era is dripping with newspaper pages and TV channels dedicated to those placed on a platform, it's shallow. McGregor was no different as he made it to the top. We stared and talked about him ad nauseam, but never actually knew him.

We still don't. We wanted enough to entertain us, but never to get too deep, to a place where we'd have to think. God forbid.

Back in 2013 upon first meeting him, access was easy. And he was easy-going. That changed as his bank balance grew, to the point that this book was a struggle to write at times. There was an *omertá* involving coaches and friends, family and opponents, and all for one clear reason. He was so valuable and had become so controlling and obnoxious, that to get on his wrong side would literally cost them dearly. Thus his entourage has become a band of yes men and women in fear of him, which drags him further down.

Where is the bottom of this pit? Maybe there is no bottom to this pit.

A number of years ago in my home town of Athy in the Irish midlands, I went to interview the snooker legend Jimmy White. He was there playing an exhibition against the late Alex Higgins and, looking back, what they became in their own right is the junction McGregor today finds himself at.

White had been a wild man and a serious user of booze and cocaine, suffered depression and, at times, stepped into madness. One night after his brother had died, he told me, he was drinking across the road when a mix of emotion and alcohol eventually became too much. He broke into the funeral home, took his brother's corpse from the coffin, sat it beside him at the bar with a top hat, and started a conversation.

A few hours later he was in a taxi taking that body to a nightclub with him, when the driver contacted the police. He had reached a complete low, a stage in his life that saw him clean himself up. He has since became insightful and fascinating on psychology and where life can takes us and how to get back.

That's one route for McGregor.

Salvation.

The other? Destruction.

That evening there was a panic as Higgins never showed up and a search through the bars and back streets began. He was eventually found asleep on the floor of a bookies covered in a mix of urine and beer. He played, but out of his mind, and at one point he threatened a child in the crowd for making noises as he lined up a shot, and a riot nearly began when the boy's father warned Higgins he'd fracture his skull with the cue ball if needed be.

Thus McGregor's future is scarily fascinating. As his past has been.

The route to now is an extraordinary one, full of fault and fallacy.

A bullied child that was told he'd amount to nothing because of what he was born into, long before he even knew what he was born into. Yet to see him stand on a Vegas stage and command a crowd is gripping and intoxicating. But scratch at the surface and there's the demise of a human behind it all.

These days, what's left of him is noise, a band of organised-crime clingers on, court appearances, and an uncertainty around a future he once took complete control of. There's a huge bank balance too, and all the trappings of fame. But sporting immortality? That's highly questionable. On the date of publication – 12 November 2019 – he will have gone three years to the day since his last win in the octagon.

This book aims to delve into all of that.

Split into two, this book is set between Las Vegas in 2018 and Dublin in 2019. One a seedy and sordid place that has at times both saved him and deluded him. The other a tough old town that once made him and now threatens to break him.

This is how I'll try and explain Conor McGregor to my nephew.

For he was a perfect man for this time and place.

The ultimate representation of a sorry society we created.

Ewan MacKenna, October 2019

CHAPTER 1

I COULD'VE BEEN A CONTENDER

THE MAN SITTING AT THE BAR HAS THE HAGGARD
face and the dirty, matted hair of someone with a past well worth
hearing about. It's the sharp, acidic aftershave that first grabs hold of
the senses and causes a twist of the head, but then sight quickly takes
over.

Each furrow on his brow is an unwanted reminder of a night out
that was too good, or a day in that wasn't good enough, but both have
resulted in him ending up here and now.

A character with a story to tell, surely. That is, until he starts to tell
it.

It's a dive of a place, just off the Las Vegas strip, in the shadow of
the Flamingo casino, with cheap beers making up for the grim and

cramped surrounds. The clientele is mostly a mix of prostitutes who've been driven away from the high rollers and fancier digs by the new and fresh desperation of those with youth on their side, and a sad and sordid sort who wish they could afford them for just an hour of less loneliness.

It's like peeling back the veneer of this city and seeing the rancid cancer it both feeds off and thrives on.

The man suddenly leaps from the stool, excited by a history he's invented, and spouts it with the belief of someone whose brain actually accepts each word that's spat out in real time. The waitress clad in hot pants rolls her eyes as she knows this routine too well. All that changes weekly is the varying depths of his plunge into madness. What remains the same is the twenty flung down hard with confidence for the first $1 bottle of booze but, as the words become slurred and the stumbling begins, even the tips start to dry up.

First on his agenda is what brought him here. He says he ran a couple of art galleries a few hours down the road in Los Angeles but got in with the Mexican cartels who started using his businesses to launder the proceeds of their cocaine sales. When it got too dangerous he simply had to get out of dodge. But it's okay, he assures those around him who have shown no evidence of any interest, let alone some semblance of concern: his house is nice and when the NFL's Oakland Raiders move to town, it'll only appreciate and he'll be back to a financial standing where he once was and always belonged.

'And I started writing my autobiography,' he continues.

Heads around immediately look towards the floor, in the hope it might actually open up. He's never heard the saying that everyone has a book in them but not everyone wants to read it. 'It was only supposed to be a one-off, but I quickly realised the life I lived should be a two-parter. I genuinely think it should be a film also, that's where the big bucks are. I've been meaning to get back to LA when the heat dies down, to talk to the studios.'

By now, the cigarette in his left hand has burnt itself into a long tube of ash which breaks off, landing in a plume on the phone charger he's plugged in beside one of the poker machines dotting the counter. He sits back down. Brushing the dust away, remembering his mobile is with him, that's something else to brag about. One more line of delusion.

'Come here, you gotta see this,' he says. And so, he pulls up his Facebook account on the screen and goes to the page of a woman that's recently added him, one that's clearly a bot. She claims to be Brazilian, has two other friends, and a single photo that amounts to a body shot from behind of a bikini-clad model on a beach looking out at a wall of beautiful blue.

'See that,' he remarks, jabbing at the screen, unperturbed. 'The sand. It's clearly Brazil. She's onto me all of the time. I gotta get down there and fuck that for a while'

Funny.

Then tragic.

Eventually exhausting.

There's a big difference between making it to Las Vegas and making it in Las Vegas.

Conor McGregor has made it here, though. For all the flak he gets, that's quite an achievement for someone born into a working-class straitjacket that tries to keep you sitting at the bar while telling lies about dreams you could and should never have had. If he had taken no for an answer and hadn't kicked the door down so ruthlessly and passed on through, how easy would it have been to attribute all of the above to him?

It's still a fortnight out from his 6 October, 2018 return to the octagon via a lightweight title bout with the brilliant Russian, Khabib Nurmagomedov, at UFC 229. And despite the time to fight night and despite so much else going on in every resort and casino and venue that blankets this part of the desert, he's a star around here. Not so much Stateside as a whole, despite what he'd have you believe, for trawl the landscape and he'll never be Bono. In fact his standing realistically lies somewhere between The Edge and The Other Two. But in Vegas, he's big news and, for all his faults, no one can ever take that from him.

At McCarran Airport, for instance, the woman at passport control upon hearing an Irish accent just assumes – correctly – it's the reason that I am here visiting. She knows.

Even before looking for payment and the obscene resort tax, the receptionist at the hotel asks when exactly the match-up takes place. He knows.

The unfortunate couple on the other side of the self-professed art dealer and international Lothario, looking to talk over him, ask for predictions. They know.

It's McGregor's town.

A taxi driver I flag down knows too, and finally gets to the details of the clash but only after the never-ending hustle and sell. A Filipino who has lived here with his wife and three kids for the best part of thirty years, he spends the first half of our journey talking about the joy of faith and of God and of children. But this is Vegas, so it's quickly down to business, the latter portent involving potential profit via presumptions and promises.

'You like massage? Happy ending? Beautiful lady?'

Both the accent and the content are like something from a Carry On movie.

Getting nowhere, he goes all in with his best line. Tried and tested.

'Bum bum,' he says, eyebrows raised. A last shot at a quick percentage of some fee.

He's bemused when his reliable go-to falls flat, but there's always the next fare. So instead, disappointed, he leaves me off outside the latest in a growing list of 'McMansions' as they've come to be known, this place built where the city stops and the oft-forgotten stunning scenery begins.

Impressive if pretentious and false, on first viewing it reminds one of the Frank Underwood line from House of Cards, and not just because of the moniker. 'Money is the McMansion in Sarasota that starts falling apart after ten years,' the Kevin Spacey character uttered early on, when the series was still good. 'Power is the old stone building that stands for centuries. I cannot respect someone who doesn't see the difference.'

It's a quote that says so much about the dwelling, and the persona of McGregor too.

There's no way inside the house, but it's here that he spends his build-up to fights in the centre of the gladiator universe. Training, eating, sleeping, like someone demented by the fact he's made it to such salubrious surrounds and doesn't want to ever let it go. Wishing you had it all is the fun part when way down there — having it, though, sees the fear of losing it take over. Wealth you imagine at the start is supposed to ease problems and not become one more. How little we know at the beginning of the journey.

This place, like all with McGregor, is heavily coated in marketing. When selected media, based on a very controlled and definitive portrayal of him as a happy-go-crazy deity, get tours of whatever is the latest rented pre-fight luxury, it has always come across as the this-is-where-the-magic-happens moment from Cribs. But those who know him and speak off the record laugh as they recount how mates and trainers often slept on lilos cramped between exercise bikes down in the basement.

In McGregor's world, perception has become the entire law, as he's lost himself to this corporate shill we always see shouting nonsense, and it's a big problem when trying to understand him.

There's so much talk that says nothing, so many looks that see nothing. To get through it all and into the clear can be as hard as passing through the mangrove.

Right now, though, that's been put on hold. Finally he's an athlete again, returned to his natural habitat, where he's contented and has a definitive beginning, middle, and end. The gates of the 'McMansion' have been slid closed, as has his mouth for the most part. Thankfully. A countdown is on to what he does best, to what used to define him so well.

Those who've witnessed him train or who have even seen his 2017 documentary, *Notorious*, that mostly amounted to a bleached and sanitised view of a troubled character, can testify to that. Behind the scenes, it was at times chaotic as he fell out with producer Patrick Timmons Ward over direction. He had it in his mind that it would be about battling back from injury to win an interim belt, but Ward was having none of it, at one stage roaring that the premise of a film could not be about a man and his knee. McGregor was baffled when stood up to. That just didn't happen anymore. However, some of the real takeaway moments that were clearly authentic and insightful centred around training and frightening dedication. Always pushing himself harder and further, like clips of him being held down and punched in the stomach for a few more seconds than the previous occasion, before one more manic burst of sit-ups.

Inch by inch, play by play, till we're finished. We are in hell right now, gentlemen. Believe me. And we can stay here and get the shit kicked out of us, or we can fight our way back into the light. We can climb out of hell.

That speech was never meant for him or his sport but it fits when he's at his driven best. One inch at a time. Always learning, too. From prior mistakes, and from what he never knew within his art. It really has been far too long since he's done what he's so good at.

This side of McGregor is like opening the windows in a stodgy old room. A fresh breeze. For the last couple of years — aside from being pockmarked with a freak show and circus act against Floyd Mayweather Jr that proved no more than you could slickly package faeces and find a seriously profitable market across the general populous these days — he's slowly and steadily become less and less of an artist and more and more of a Kardashian.

Famous for being famous.

The terrifying minute there's a threat of silence, as if a bad thing, there's a need to interject with controversy. Always staying relevant by lowering the bar. In other words, a quintessential modern guide to becoming empty and rich. Money first, morality never.

Here's a small snippet from the ever-growing rap sheet that has come to define him.

April 2017. McGregor turns up at the Grand National at Aintree with his shirt open despite the chilled air, the lenses on his glasses open like sun roofs despite no clouds in the sky, and tellingly the makings of a gut plunging out for all to see. Mayhem ensued. A rental business had a go at him for jumping on the bonnet of a Rolls Royce, with a company executive adding, 'He is stood on the car acting like it is his own. It is not his own.' It's a beginning to his five-day session on Merseyside, rather than an end, with headlines emerging about making it rain with banknotes at a nightclub, being challenged to a fight by a bouncer, crashing a random house party, getting his hand slashed open, rumours of a bill for damage to a hotel room, and eventually public allegations and claims from a new mother around him getting her pregnant and her having his child. By the end, his Instagram is led by a shot of him sitting on a private jet with an open bag full of cash, looking like Father Jack in the Competition Time episode of Father Ted.

November 2017. Front row at a Bellator event in Dublin, McGregor jumps into the cage to celebrate teammate Charlie Ward's win. It was before referee Marc Goddard was finished and before the medical team had begun, and he went for the official and shoved the defeated John Redmond back down onto the canvas. Soon, he was sitting on the side of the octagon, slapped a commissioner, did laps of the ring before a bemused crowd, and eventually left for his hotel, where reports emerged that police were called.

April 2018. McGregor and his mates hop onto a private jet from Dublin in what seemed and still seems a UFC marketing act gone wrong. It's a little complicated, but the dumbed-down version goes like this: his friend and teammate, Russia's Artem Lobov, had run into Khabib in a hotel lobby in the Big Apple, where a combination of McGregor allegiance, Dagestan-Russian tension, along with far too much testosterone, saw an inevitable bust-up occur. Getting wind of the news, McGregor took to the skies in a rage and upon landing, his entourage, in security obsessed post-9/11 New York, strolled straight into the Barclays Centre where they met no guards but cameramen, and meandered all the way to where the athletes including Khabib were boarding a bus. It's there he and his mates went too far, smashing windows and injuring some of those on board with shards of glass. Eventually it ended up in court.

There have been court appearances in Ireland, too: taunting of judges with late shows, speeding off from speeding hearings. He's been a mess of a person, egged on by yes-men and pushing whatever admirable memories of him that once existed further down the rabbit hole. There are endless clips which hint at excess and debauchery. Everybody's seen them and read the commentary, because everybody has WhatsApp — from Conor asleep in a ditch to more cheap and spicy claims under internet headlines about women.

This is what happens when the painter doesn't paint, when the writer doesn't write, when the sculptor doesn't sculpt. And when the fighter doesn't fight. The discipline keeps McGregor sane, and he needs it like a drug. When he's chasing something, he's his own worst enemy and best friend, because any boast roared into a microphone has to be backed up. He's scared he cannot do what he says, while never knowing what he will say. It turns him into an addict of a different sort as he immerses himself, so he can say he told you so through a cheeky grin, his hands held aloft. It has created this MMA athlete few are like, as it's ballet when he dances on his canvas.

It also means the fighter in his element is all that's recognisable from the kid who started this unlikely trip, who signed up to it without knowing or asking, 'What next?' It's been hard for others in different eras to make a jump from nothing to everything, so just imagine Mickey Mantle starting his career with the backslapping writers on the train, and ending it with TMZ chasing him through the streets. It's disorientating and makes it difficult to tread the fine line between excuses, ownership of wrong, and distribution of blame. Not that there's a shortage of the latter to go around.

To fans. To media. To him.

That's too deep, though. Locally, the burning question is instead whether he can come back from the madness and whatever toll his lifestyle has taken on his body and mind in recent years.

That question is what the bookmakers are considering with his upcoming fight, but the real wonder that few consider is what happens to him if this is where the athlete ends. What kind of person has this adventure left behind once the chaos has ended? Has it hollowed him out from the inside and, if so, what comes next for the sorry shell?

There's little time to ponder it tonight, though.

The sharp, acidic aftershave wafts into the nostrils again. A glance up and the man in the bar is wandering back. The cigarette has been replaced with his waving of that mobile so big that anyone nearby can clearly see the screensaver: the most graphic shot you could imagine from a hardcore porn magazine. When does it go wrong to the point that this is the coping mechanism?

There's a big difference between making it to Las Vegas and making it in Las Vegas.

CHAPTER 2

IT'S A DIRTY OLD TOWN

THE MAN SITTING AT THE BAR LEANS LAZILY WAY back in his stool, his gut almost resting beside his pint on the counter by the time of maximum recline. It's January 2019, and there's a decent crowd in the Black Forge Inn on Drimnagh Road, manning the fort early on a Monday morning.

Some with money to burn will use this scene as proof that the boom and the good times have returned to Ireland. Those who know the truth will tell you it's proof of the opposite, a simple escape from the reality of being a have-not in a city with loud and louder haves.

The man glances over a few times, hoping to catch an eye. All alone, it's easy to tell he's itching just to make conversation. Glancing back, though, the curiosity is whether the cherry-red face is from the slap of the vicious winter air outside or from the drink flowing inside. He answers indirectly.

Dragging himself forward, he says that over the holidays his doctor told him to cut out alcohol due to some serious heart issues. He takes a large slurp from his glass, coughs, exhales, and says he'd rather be dead than to miss out on this.

This?

Of course, this is also where Conor McGregor used to drink and still does occasionally. This is where so many quips and tales and stories and truths about him both start and end.

Perhaps it was age; perhaps it was the miles on the clock; perhaps it was the lifestyle he'd slipped into for a little too long; perhaps it was simply that the hunger had been plenty fed. After all, getting into a cage and trying to take another man's consciousness isn't a natural thing to engage in for a living, never mind when you've made the money to completely avoid it. But a few months have passed since he was beaten up by Khabib Nurmagomedov in their title fight, eventually submitting in round four, having made it that far by just dragging out the inevitable conclusion, such was the gulf in class.

Since then, back at home here, he's again reverted from the back pages to the front pages. As if the hero of Greek tragedy brought down by a combination of the world's pressures and the flaws in his own troubled and, at times, tortured personality.

It's long become a habit of his, one that the voyeuristic public that once roared him on are drawn to as if rubbernecking at a mangled car and its bloody victims. There's a trend around those we place on a pedestal: cheer someone on the way up in the name of entertainment, but when that act grows stale, it's time for a different kind of amusement. More and more we lust after that ending to fill the void in ourselves via the faults of others.

Over Christmas, there's been the usual rumours and hard news that follow him like a dark, dreary shadow. A leaked plan for the morning radio show of the national broadcaster, RTÉ, lets social media in on the worst-kept secret in these parts.

NB NB Not for publication/Broadcast NB NB Conor McGregor presented himself to Garda at 5pm yesterday in connection with a recent assault allegation in the city. Garda have 24 hours to question the MMA fighter. NB Consult Morning Editor for 'DIRECTION'.

No charges have yet been brought against him.

There's the constant stream of videos on social media as well, of him pulling up to this and that apartment in the rougher and tougher parts of the capital, insinuations about the purposes for these visits, claims that the reason he looks the worse for wear in photos that emerge is because he's strung out. This is always highlighted by the contrast with him when he's in camp, as his skin loses that glorious glow and muscles give way to either flab or to bone.

A tweet from a member of the press on a stakeout starkly reads that an 'international sports star… has recently spent a 36hr period in a known crack cocaine den in a flat complex in the South Inner City. A change of clothes was brought in for the person.'

Clawing after every detail.

There's no proof that this was in any way true, other than a recording taken via a hidden camera at some distance. Think about this logically: the person in the clip certainly looks like him, as they get out of the type of car he cruises around in. And to manipulate that entire situation if it wasn't him, while setting up a camera in a flat nearby, seems crazier than any idea of him being there.

If that and the entire story is real, then it's a sorry twist. Just picture it.

The guy who had it all, in a grimy apartment where damp climbs walls, with bare and dirty mattresses instead of furniture waiting for the next corpse to fall onto them. If this ever was the case, it's as if he withdrew from the world because it wouldn't withdraw from him. Again, none of this has been nailed down as fact, but many make claims, with public figures like Paulie Malignaggi making insinuations about his conduct out of the octagon.

While he can seem so unique and unusual at times, such behaviour wouldn't be unique or unusual. In fact, it's a well-worn walk for many rich and famous in and out of sport.

His entourage, according to those who have been close to it, is always overly concerned with keeping him happy. If someone says something he doesn't like, it gets brought up. He's loud; everything moves to his beat. Once, in 2015, those new to the scene got a taste when, at four in the afternoon, he walked into the living room of the McMansion in just his boxers and started shouting about how he was the greatest. His constant thinking is that if he carries himself like a king and a champion, then he is a king and a champion.

Sometimes.

Sometimes, he couldn't be further from such descriptions, but he keeps shouting what becomes delusion. As Fyodor Dostoevsky said, 'The man who lies to himself and listens to his own lie comes to a point that he cannot distinguish the truth within him, or around him, and so loses all respect for himself and for others. And having no respect he ceases to love.' How awfully apt.

Not liking those that disagree with him may no longer be his most grave fault, but it is the root cause of so many other faults. No one will stand up to him for his own good, because so many are on the payroll. Some are milking him, and it makes it hard for him to recognise who his friends are — this from a situation of high paranoia to begin with. One pal runs The Mac Life website. The latest story from a source is that another has allegedly gotten a job that involves looking after his hipster socks. It's more tragedy than comedy.

'It's why I hate even talking about his links,' says one person close to him. 'Everything you say seems so ridiculous, but it's true. We are talking about a lad from Crumlin here,' they add, referring to the relatively working-class part of Dublin looked down on by those from leafier climes, and occasionally run down by McGregor as well to add to the gangster image he chases after.

There's been lighter gossip here in Dublin this January, too. One story doing the rounds has been that he bought this pub, but the man at the bar puts out that fire. He does it with the curt honesty of local speak as well. 'Complete bollocks,' he grunts and starts up on McGregor talk without any prompting. 'They said he was in here before Christmas as well, and that he spent four bleedin' grand. Four grand? He did in his hoop. He was in here with about twenty mates and a load of security – big Polish heads – over there in the corner, and all they did was drink his whiskey for nothing. They wouldn't even have the decency to go into the jacks to do their lines. Right here on the fuckin' bar.'

Myth and reality have become one, it seems, in a fascination with celebrity, with someone who made it out but keeps on coming back.

The philosophising about him is cut short, however, when another regular rushes into the Black Forge. He's found an open eight-pack of Duracell A++ batteries outside on the ground, with only one missing. Excited, he wonders if they still work, which begins a debate as to why they wouldn't. With that, he starts to share the bounty around.

All the while, the echoes inside insinuate what McGregor's become. His highs and his lows, his expertise and his flaws, in and out of the octagon, have created a chaos, a never-ending attraction, an enchantment about him that doesn't need his presence to exist.

Where did it all go right?

Where did it all go wrong?

It's about a twelve-minute drive from here to the Straight Blast Gym, a bunker in the corner of an industrial estate, a constant reminder that in this business, substance makes you and style breaks you. Think back some thirty years to Cuban physical instructor Nicholas Cruz. After defecting, he ended up in Ireland, running the national boxing programme. At one stage, he took the team to Kerry for a training camp but found nothing except for a ring on the ground floor of the hotel. In the end, he borrowed a sledgehammer and tyre from a nearby farmyard and used them for cardio and strength work. He smashed rocks and used the smaller pieces as dumbbells; he used trees for chin-ups; and he had his team doing squats up and down the dunes on a beach. Then he went looking for a masseuse to the amusement of higher powers. By the 1992 Olympics, Ireland came home with both a gold and a silver medal. Time moves on, but in combat sports methodology, it doesn't always. It's quite simple for the most part.

Straight Blast Gym has served McGregor plenty well. It's where he trained so brutally and brilliantly to make it. His sanctuary and salvation all in one, like that one pub where you never ask for the Wi-fi code, as instead you go there to read and to watch the world. Any outside intrusions would ruin that.

It's a couple of minutes less to the McDonald's where we first met in early 2013. The choice of venue was his after his maiden UFC victory, a first-round stoppage of Marcus Brimage who had called McGregor 'an arrogant person that needs a reality check'. His inability to miss the chin earned him knockout of the night and, more importantly, the $60,000 that came with it. A figure that would be swallowed up by the sums he earns now for just showing his face for a split second, it meant everything to him back then.

The tape of our chat is still in a drawer, and taking it out on occasion brings back memories. In the car park that day, there was a warmth coming off McGregor. It seemed the impossible had happened, but as he spoke, he showed how he had made it possible.

'Even before this, all the problems I'd have in life, when I'd go to the gym, they were gone,' he said at the time. 'I used it as an escape, that's why I was there eight hours a day. It's the way it's always been, and that's why I do it. I can escape from everything. It's hard to explain. The fact I'm such a believer in your thoughts becoming reality now, it makes me realise that back in the day, I was always thinking about danger and I ended up bringing it. They were my first lessons in the law of attraction.

'But you have to be obsessed. If you talk to me about football, I wouldn't have a clue what you're on about. If you're talking to me about energy efficiency from the bottom position, we can talk into next week. I don't know what's what, but I know how to break down the human frame no matter the size. And I know how positive thinking matters.'

That law of attraction means a positive or negative outlook results in a similar outcome, and it was just one of the philosophies of both body and mind he was absorbing.

Freestyle wrestling, Thai boxing, even his first flirtation with capoeira — the Brazilian fight dance, he explained, that originated with African slaves who didn't want their masters to know they were training so they disguised it as rhythmic movement. It was hard not to be drawn into how he picked apart a game that many see as barbaric, making it sound like chess as he studied anything and everything to improve himself and his chances.

'If you dedicate yourself to one style, you best believe you are weak at another discipline,' he added. 'I like to be able to move every way. There's a time and place for all disciplines. I study all different styles, and there's no limit to where the body can move to attack and defend. The more movements your body can make in a combat situation, the more your opponent is put on the back foot and is reacting to your movements rather than creating his own movements. I learn from anything. I saw two gorillas on television play fighting. Crazy stuff.

It's like freestyle wrestling. They are arm dragging, and their posture is so solid — and posture for combat is so vital. I even take from them.'

He hadn't cashed the $60,000 at that stage, the biggest amount he'd seen and simply too much to have really imagined. But McDonald's wasn't about the present, instead it was a promise he wouldn't change in the future. After all, he'd always treated himself to a weekly cup of coffee there, and this was no different. There was a glint in his eye, an accessible giddiness, a likeable roguishness.

He'd been in the social welfare queue not long before. He'd also applied for a job in the bookmaker, BoyleSports, and was turned down, and next they were coming calling to try and sponsor him. So much seemed the perfect story, but how often do the great tales end on a high?

At one point, he'd even told his old man that if left to his own devices, he'd be a millionaire by the time he was 25. 'They were always onto me,' he recalled of his parents. '"You aren't doing anything productive with your life, you need to go and get a job." I had some tough times with my Da. "Get your arse into a fucking job. What are you doing? You're doing nothing with your life." I had to listen to it all the time, right up to two months ago. But in Ireland, it's a rush to work, that's the wrong way. I was thrown into a plumbing apprenticeship. I hated it, fifteen-hour days, just getting bossed around.

'I just decided, fuck this. I'd have a go at MMA. Honestly, I'd rather be poor. I'd rather have no money and just be training than in a job I don't love. I don't get that. If someone asked me for advice about work, if you're in a job you don't love, just quit. You only live once and you want to chase what you want to chase. People in Ireland, all over the world, they have that negative mindset. They focus on what if something bad happens. That's no way to live. Think what happens when it goes right. Why worry? It'll only bring more worry. When you focus on the positive, the negative shrinks away. What you think about, then it will happen. You are never wrong, and that's just what I believe in.'

A certain Oscar Wilde quote always comes to mind when that tape of our interview rolls. 'When I was young I thought that money was the most important thing in life; now that I am old I know that it is.' As for of all the thoughts he shared that day, one sends a shiver and stays lurking.

'I told everyone I'd do it, but they never believed me,' he smirked without a care. 'Now look at me. But people say be careful of the money, don't blow it. If the money becomes a problem, I'll get rid of it. I've been planning to get to this stage for a long, long time and I won't let anything stop me. Honestly. And there's so much going on and so many people trying to get in touch, I just go to the gym. It's the place I can forget everything.'

They say the past is like a foreign country. They do things differently there. As for this country, this present, he lives by the ideal that there's more to life than money, but money can buy that for him, too.

Maybe the gym is the place he can still forget the lot, but look at the tall mound of problems and issues he must leave outside every time he enters. Back then, he smiled at water under the bridge — probably because it had passed underneath and was gone — laughed at his present, and was wide-eyed about the future. Be careful what you wish for.

Being shunted into fame and fortune might make you initially, but ultimately it will try and break you as well. It didn't even take that long for McGregor: back in 2013, after the McDonald's coffee, he called his girlfriend Dee after training and begged her for a lift home in a banged-up car. He simply didn't fancy the few miles on foot.

Within two years though, by 2015, he was on ESPN, playing up to a wretched persona. Asked about his love life, he couldn't control his response as the parody had already overtaken him, and he was only thinking of his image. 'I've a long-term girlfriend,' he boasted. 'I don't know about romance, but I like to get down occasionally. I don't really have a romantic side is what I am saying. If I'm going in, I'm going in for the kill. You won't catch me walking down the beach holding hands; you will catch me going deep.'

What did she think as he began to change? Did she try to stop it occurring?

What did he think as he began to change? Did he notice? Did he care?

By then, the glint in his eye, the accessible giddiness, the likeable roguishness, were gone.

When God wants to punish us, he answers our prayers.

CHAPTER 3

GEAR AND GOADING IN LAS VEGAS

WHEN COCAINE IS SNORTED INTO THE NOSTRIL, A scientifically fascinating and physiologically joyous process rapidly begins to occur. Quickly mixing with mucus, the substance finds a way into the blood vessels in the walls of your nose. This is the access point to the entire body and to what some say is sheer bliss in little more than an instant.

Travelling the highways and byways that are the arteries, the drug is transported from the toes all the way to, crucially, the crown of the head. That's quite remarkable, because in order to get there, the particles have to find a way past the highly selective blood-brain barrier which is in place to separate the circulating blood, the extracellular fluid in the central nervous system, and the brain itself. Basically, it's a fail-safe designed to keep you from dying a painful death.

To get past said barrier, the substance unlocks the security mechanism by essentially scrambling the code. This of course opens up the brain to intrusion from all sorts of other toxins that should never get near it and can have long-term debilitating effects, from Alzheimer's to Parkinson's, from MS to neuroAIDS.

But hey, you're here for a good time, not a long time, right?

And once in your brain, the cocaine starts playing great tricks. The key element as far as the high is concerned is not only the release of the happy chemical, dopamine, in large quantities but also the type of dopamine produced. When created normally, it returns to the site of its production and is recycled. But under the influence, that doesn't happen. Instead, it floods and submerges the cells all the way across your body.

Your temperature increases.

Your blood pressure goes up.

Your appetite disappears.

Your energy grows.

You become untouchable.

The guy wrapped in the tricolour at the bathroom counter in the Park MGM on the Las Vegas strip snaps his head upwards in a rush. His pupils dilate and his eyes roll back in his skull as he's clearly in the midst of getting that sensation. It's not hard to tell that he already feels invincible.

Slowly this late September of 2018, the Irish have arrived into Nevada like a trickle of contaminated water and, even in small, early numbers, they make their presence felt. From this moment on, those of us here to cover the McGregor-Khabib fight start being more cautious with our passports. A glimpse from the locals and there's instant association with those here to tear it up for just a little while – and not in the relatively refined way Americans do when claiming to party or blow out.

For so long now, we've been hearing about a new and more confident generation coming from Ireland, to the point that it's actually straddled across several generations of Irish. Each one going that small bit further to the point that such unheralded confidence has long been traded for insufferable arrogance. As a people, we're under the impression that everyone loves us, and they might have done once. But some rightly feel that it would be great if we were a tad more reticent.

Two chances over the coming days.

This guy is one of the first to make it, giving himself a decent stint in the city. Thus he has a hotel. A smattering of those that usually come late on the Thursday so they can take in a weigh-in and fight before jetting off come Sunday don't always check-in anywhere. They avoid sleep on a diet of drink, drugs, and McGregor — a concoction that adds to already giant egos.

So many are the same as each other, and the same as their hero.

They dress like him.

They cut their hair like him.

They wear their shades like him.

They grow their beards like him.

They talk like him.

The late philosopher Denis Dutton once said: 'Dumbing down takes many forms. Art that is good for you, museums that flatter you, universities that increase your self-esteem. Culture, after all, is really about you.' In 2018, McGregor is a form of culture. And while it's annoying just to see such a phenomenon, that's what he is for MMA. It doesn't make the sports pages in Ireland, instead he makes them.

Or at least that's what it was, as the numbers have fallen off a little in recent times, as he's become better known for his antics and actions outside of the octagon. And why wouldn't he be, given it's so long since he's been in it? If his December 2015 destruction of the seemingly untouchable Brazilian José Aldo — when he knocked out the guy many believed to be one of the all-time greats in a mere thirteen seconds to become UFC champion — created the legend and the icon, that's fast becoming a memory so distant it's in danger of blurring into fiction. Back then, for those of us with issues about his words and his use of his exploding fame, what made it worse was that despite the long line of asterisks, he was like Duke basketball's elitism, Alex Ferguson's unerring and tiresome dominance at Old Trafford, or the New England Patriots and all their shady episodes.

He kept on winning, backing up his words and shutting down so much deserved criticism and undeserved negativity.

It was then that a petition started circulating to get his face on actual legal tender, and it had so many signatures as to be debated by the government. 'It would be a true honour for me to be immortalised on the €1 coin!' McGregor wrote on Facebook. 'Thank you to my fans for the petition! Let's go Oireachtas!' Politicians eventually deemed it inadmissible as it would have needed pan-European support, but it was a peek into the madness.

There was always a nastiness that oozed from the mob, too. Any time you stepped out of line and dared to critique McGregor or the UFC itself in anything other than pandering terms, you could expect to be met with an abusive reaction, insisting you clearly didn't know what you were talking about. Platforms like Twitter have only made things worse: the entire idea of social media is to open you up to other viewpoints, not make you more entrenched, but those who follow sport are averse to any criticism.

For years, you couldn't utter so much as a bad word without those replies; replies that showed both a laziness and the lack of a proper counterpoint. No matter how wrong his behaviour and no matter how valid our reasons for questioning it, we weren't supposed to do anything but giggle at McGregor's infantile quips. You were dubbed negative, a begrudger, called out for jealously and bitterness. Passport colour was mentioned too, as if where someone is from rather than what they do should be a cause for admiration. As the great comedian George Carlin best put it, 'Pride should be reserved for something you achieve or obtain on your own, not something that happens by accident of birth. Being Irish isn't a skill, it's a fucking genetic accident. You wouldn't say I'm proud to be 5'11; I'm proud to have a pre-disposition for colon cancer.'

And then, to show that so much of their behaviour was learned and copied, fans belched out the standard line of 'educate yourself on MMA'. That summed up the misplaced attraction to their god, for McGregor shouldn't be mostly about his sport. He's bigger and far more fascinating beyond its boundaries. To focus solely on the profession would be like limiting thoughts on Tiger Woods to his swing or Johnny Manziel to his arm strength.

Curious about such cultishness and this era of hero worship, I spoke to Orin Starn before my trip to Vegas. A professor at the prestigious Duke University in North Carolina, one of his books was *The Passion of Tiger Woods: An Anthropologist Reports on Golf, Race, and Celebrity Scandal*, which explored the golfer's place in US culture and society.

'Certainly showmanship, a big mouth, and a brash style have always been part of sporting celebrity going back to Jack Johnson, or maybe Achilles,' Starn noted. 'There are greater marketing opportunities now, though, and in such a dog-eat-dog world of Twitter accounts and craziness of all kinds, a guy that's willing to say what he thinks and to cut a brash, macho persona is a marketable figure. All the boxes are ticked with McGregor. Being rude, brawling, saying what you think no matter how hateful, is all back in fashion. It all works.

'The other thing that strikes me when looking at him, is that it's also the age and return of that macho man. It's no coincidence in this time of Trump, Erdoğan, Bolsonaro, and Putin. They are all male, and there is this discourse of the strong man that will impose his will on history. So there's an appetite for the strong man that doesn't shy away from the fight, and McGregor fits that bill within sport.

'To me, it really is more the idea of the charismatic strongman that's crucially linked up to elements of and the surge in right-wing populism. I can see why McGregor could be an object of that adoration.

'On top of that we have seen, partly in response to the global return of xenophobia, racism, hate, and cheap populism, there has been a revival of the 1960s and 1970s-type activist athlete. They speak out about social issues. LeBron James. Colin Kaepernick. The Conor McGregor attitude, however, is different. It's all about the dollar and performance, and because of that, in some ways it's a departure, or at least a different pathway through the modern sporting landscape. A move away from the embrace of social responsibility.'

There are those who have had enough of that kind of spectacle, and many of the names on the coin petition have grown tired of the creation, but many more do still continue to cling to and exude their hero's sense of entitlement and the notion that everyone wants in on their brand of loud banter. However, as stunning and fast his rise on the canvas has been, his deterioration into caricature, falsity, and child-ishness has also happened at breakneck speed. And as much as he's grown as a fighter, he's shrunk as a sports star to whom people can look up and admire.

Yet, these here in the Park MGM in Vegas do admire him.

They let everyone know.

As Irish, were we like this at Italia '90, forcing 'craic' on others there to enjoy the World Cup? Hopefully not, because if there is a crucial difference between now and then, it was the humility coming off the back of a brutal decade of deprivation, decline, and misery. Such hardship does a lot to a people's natural sense of place in the global pecking order. Nearly thirty years on, though, and we have a group coming through right after the boom that caused the belt of the economy to stretch, buckle, and finally snap across much of the 2000s.

It was a situation that allowed those who had it to flaunt it proudly in a previously reserved society. Celebrity sections of papers expanded to incorporate odious, widely known property developers, who where somehow admired for their irresponsible greed. The country had a Miss World in Rosanna Davison, who once had on-duty police down tools in the snow so they could get her from a club to her home, because that's where their and our priorities lay for a stint. Teachers and nurses bought second and third properties in Bulgaria and Spain, even Abu Dhabi and Dubai. There were instances when what once were regular house parties had actual GPS co-ordinates on the invitation in case you were going by helicopter. The Taoiseach Bertie Ahern suggested that those saying the bubble would soon burst should contemplate topping themselves.

In a way, McGregor's attitude and by extension that of his fans captures that era: crucially, it was a time that brought about an accepted thinking whereby end profit justified moral means, as the bank balance was a man's one and only measure.

* * *

NEVER MIX PLEASURE WITH BUSINESS?

With Conor McGregor, it's been impossible not to.

The fan phenomenon might be an oddity that intrigues on the surface level, but beneath that, he's also seriously profitable. If the Dubliner clearly had a talent for the sport, it didn't take long for the UFC and particularly Dana White to see he had a talent for driving income as well. More than any moments on the canvas, this is why they not only tolerate but indulge a guy who crosses the boundaries of a business notorious for the strict and often cynical and downright nasty treatment of its fighters.

It's why to talk about the UFC as a whole while trying to avoid McGregor is to not fully understand how bad it could've been for them.

And how good it is for them.

Kurt Badenhausen, a senior editor at *Forbes* who has looked at the business dealings of the UFC closely, is quick to back this up. 'I don't think Conor's importance was ever overstated,' he notes of a guy overhyped in strictly fighting terms. 'He is driving numbers that never before existed, and you see the impact that he had versus the rest. He is the top guy by a long way. He's obviously the biggest star and drives the biggest pay-per-view numbers, and it's been that way for a while. But with the UFC, it's somewhat of a black box, and they keep everything pretty close to their chests.

'Granted, that's not unusual. It's been the way combat sports have existed since the beginning of time, as the promoter doesn't want to reveal much as in many cases it's bad optics. That promoter doesn't want people to see how little is filtering down to the fighters. Look at boxing through the 70s and 80s, even today, how they are taking advantage of fighters by keeping a sizeable chunk of the proceeds. That changed a little with Oscar De La Hoya starting his own company, and then Floyd Mayweather took it to a whole other level and really flipped the switch. But it's harder for McGregor or any UFC fighter to do that, because UFC is by far the biggest game in town. For someone to go out on their own, it's a real challenge to move out to one of these lesser MMA operations. As it stands now, you could never command the money McGregor could make in the UFC.'

Humble beginnings, maybe. But even if they tried not to see, McGregor and his team could never have shut their eyes on his true worth or where the UFC would've been without him and his mouth. In 2017, for instance, the UFC made over $700m — a record number, despite the fact they only managed 4.1 million pay-per-view buys.

What mattered, though, was the McGregor-Mayweather bout in a boxing ring in which the UFC had a massive vested interest.

For that, revenue topped the $600m mark. Sponsorship was estimated at $22m, ticket sales came in at $77.1m via an average seat close to $4,000, and pay-per-view smashed the sweet science's previous high by adding in an estimated $455m. It didn't matter that it was like putting Mo Farah and Usain Bolt against each other in a 10-kilometre race and claiming it would be epic as they were both track stars: supporters couldn't see past the sell.

In a grim way, their naivety, ignorance and indulgence made others rich.

When I wrote an article trying to save people their wages around buying into what might as well have been a fix, such were the chances of an upset, a flood of emails and comments came back to me at the time. Surmising them was this one: 'This article was written by another butthurt, pussy snowflake, who needs to get real. What a whiny load of wank this article really is. This journalist needs to get out and get a life of his own.'

The talk of a right-wing strongman.

That in itself was proof that it's not McGregor the athlete who is all that valuable. For imagine had they thrown in another boxing nobody who had long retired and didn't stand a chance. Yet, because of his persona, people forked out £19.95 in the UK, €24.95 in Ireland, $99.99 in the United States to watch the fight in their living rooms.

It didn't matter that we had been here before in 1976, when Muhammad Ali was tempted to the pay-day as he entered into a contest with pro-wrestler Antonio Inoki. After fourteen seconds, the Japanese assumed the crab position on the canvas. Ali didn't throw a punch until the seventh as a result and threw a total of six across the full fifteen rounds as he roared 'coward' at the man crawling around. By the end, so little had occurred it was a draw.

For the few people who could afford it or those few diehards who were willing to spend money they didn't have, it didn't matter that they were handing their cash to a woman-beating American and an Irishman with friendships and links to the Dublin mafia. When the latter was asked in an interview in the lead up to the bout whether he could beat Rocky Balboa from *Rocky III*, he racked his brains: 'I'm trying to remember which one was *Rocky III*. Was that the one in the celebrity gym? I can't remember if that's the one with the dancing monkeys or not.' Days earlier he had already shouted 'dance for me boy' at Mayweather at the pair's first joint promotional appearance for the fight. Such bigoted comments didn't seem to matter anymore.

McGregor made it different.

It didn't matter that the present-day warning lights were so frequent and prominent that it looked like a nightclub. Boxrec.com rated Mayweather as the best pound-for-pound pugilist of them all, ahead of Carlos Monzon and Rocky Marciano, Marvin Hagler, Tommy Hearns, Sugar Ray Robinson and Ali. Meanwhile, McGregor had been so limited when it came to boxing that he left it behind after taking a beating in the early stages of the Irish amateur intermediate championships many years prior. As one former Irish Olympian told me when remembering his quality in that sport, 'In boxing, he couldn't and wouldn't beat eggs. But joking aside, he wasn't at the standard of even that. Today, he wouldn't even win an Irish title at his weight. That's the level.'

Still, McGregor made it different.

It didn't matter that where once loyalty was a give-and-get relationship, this bout turned it into a cul-de-sac. Desperate to be the biggest grossing event of them all, the organisers priced tickets so ridiculously high that many of McGregor's travelling fans couldn't afford them. Instead, they were forced to get their fill of him at the weigh-in and the press conference. Come the actual main event, they were left outside in the warm while inside the T-Mobile Arena, a massive bank of seats were cordoned off and left empty. Those who'd supported him all the way up suddenly didn't matter a whole lot, a sign of the greed and of the promoters having eyes far bigger than their bellies.

Still, McGregor made it different.

It didn't matter that, of the few people who could afford it or those few diehards who were willing to spend what they didn't have, they had to decide to hand over their money to a woman-beating American and an Irishman with friendships and links to the Dublin mafia, who had also come across as a racist by telling Mayweather to 'dance for me boy' while describing black people in a gym as 'dancing monkeys'. It didn't even matter the prime reason that the mismatch was signed up to was that Mayweather needed to pay a tax bill and his opponent needed attention.

Still, McGregor made it different.

It's why six weeks before that fight, in July 2017, the fans even showed up in Toronto and watched Mayweather grab an Irish flag and wrap it around his shoulders. Chest out as always, on what lazily encompassed part two of a world tour of just three stops, McGregor predictably got on the microphone and resorted to what he has become better known for than even his truly impressive MMA ability. 'If you do something with that flag, I'll fuck you up,' he said like a thuggish teen. He then took a backpack belonging to the American, pulled wads of cash from it and laughed, 'That's it? That's it? There's about five grand in here. Fuck me.' At this point, arguably the finest boxer ever squatted down and pretended to go to the toilet as the Irishman again roared with the conviction of a local am-dram actor, 'You do something with that flag I'm going to fuck you up on this stage.' It was the sort of stuff that, as kids, would cause our parents to walk into the living room, grab the remote control and turn off WWF, saying we ought to grow up.

But again McGregor made it different, once more bending the rules and the levels. It's this that Dana White has managed to exploit and profit from.

As Badenhausen says, 'Dana's best thing is that his marketing skills are tremendous. From that business standpoint, what he has done to market the UFC through hard work, force of will, just constantly being on message about what the UFC is … This has made him the most important person in the sport over the past fifteen years. He's been the constant. Fighters cycle through; he's always been there and has helped build that thing since the Fertittas brought it from a $2m to a $4bn business. Behind the bluster, he's tremendous. Sure, Conor has played his part in that, and I think McGregor has pushed back more than any fighter before him, because he's had more leverage than any fighter before him. He sees this company being sold for more than $4bn, and that's a wake-up call for a lot of people who said, "Wow, I didn't realise the money was that big."

'And he knows he's the most important asset. He's self-confident to begin with, and it made him step up and say, "I want my piece. If this is worth $4bn, what am I worth? Why am I making $7m or $8m a fight when I'm such a big piece of it?" But these things are cyclical. Fighters cycle in and out of being in the spotlight, and that means Dana White feels he's empowered to push back, too. They want to keep a very centralised system in place so they can maximise their prof-itability. And he's been doing this for so long, and it's something all sports have to tackle when a transcendent figure comes along, whether that's Tiger Woods in golf or McGregor here.

'The people who run these businesses know it's not a permanent situation and that you have to find a way to leverage it. Dana is looking ahead for the next ten years, and that won't include Conor. It's part of the natural cycle.

'There'll be another fighter that captures the imagination of the public; maybe he's already out there. But for now, of course, Dana allows Conor more leeway while he is here. Special treatment. There's different rules for different people across all business. If you are the guy that's driving the train in terms of generating revenue, then you're going to have some more flexibility. Dana White has spoken about that, when he's forced certain fighters to do certain things in terms of promotions but has given Conor more slack. But not everything. He makes it very clear Conor has a contract with the UFC and works for him, and that he has to be reminded. But without a doubt he gets more slack. He's the alpha dog for the sport, and he's a tremendous cash cow for the sport.'

Beyond that, he's an anomaly in the sport. Even if it is nascent and still feeling its way.

It's why the media around MMA are tentative and unsure how to react to him, while the media outside MMA often don't realise just how big he is for the sport. If you have next to no interest, which is the vast majority, and are asked to name an MMA fighter, you'll say him. But then who? Relatively, he isn't quite Michael Jordan in that he's not the greatest ever, even if he's in the top few percentiles as regards to ability and achievement. But he's an icon like Jordan in UFC terms. Every sponsor and business want him, and he's pushing the boat out. In 2016, when he briefly retired, he said it was because he didn't want to do a press conference as he should be paid separately for giving up time. That's the power.

Will there be another like him?

Right now, it's hard to imagine, but that's the problem with the present. Not long ago, the writer Thomas Hauser described the WME-IMG $4.2bn purchase of UFC as 'starting to look like Time Warner's decision to merge with AOL'. Yet soon the valuation went up on that, even if the quality came down. No one could have predicted that would come next.

As one person near the UFC says off the record, 'Go back and look at that Reebok deal. It was to dress up this company and to make this look like a real sport, for there was a lot of complaining about the brutality and so on from more mainstream sports media. There was the anti-doping, there was that. But then they go and sell it for €4bn, and look at where it is now. That idea went out the window. Instead, you have Brock Lesnar and Daniel Cormier doing pro-wrestling-style skits in the ring. Before, they couldn't have done that. McGregor's profitability and how he makes them money is a key factor in that. Now, there are interim titles every week to sell pay-per-views to customers who lap it up. They change rankings to suit when a fight is coming — a guy is not ranked, two weeks before the event he appears at fourteen. It is crazy, and the sport I knew is gone. They make titles for no reason other than numbers falling, behind the odd event like McGregor-Mayweather hiding reality. And with that, they know how vital Conor is. Dana said on ESPN that he's the greatest ever. That is absurd to anyone that knows the sport. He's not George St-Pierre. It's the most valuable conflated with best ever for profit.'

In essence, it's like the Trump model: say it and it becomes a headline, and that headline soon becomes real. The winners are the UFC.

* * *

'THE GREATEST,' COMES THE ROAR.

The guy from the Park MGM toilets rejoins his friends outside for a drink. Any good words the UFC have ever marketed around their man, they've been all ears. If he's the best, then it makes them associated with the best and that allows notions to abound.

Some years ago back in Ireland, the Celtic Tiger was slayed, even if it bore a more recent and equally vile offspring. But McGregor and his supporters are a constant reminder of what self-admiration does to a nation.

On this latest McGregor binge, they are a man down. But it wasn't like 2015 and the Aldo fight when JetBlue flight 611, leaving New York for Vegas, taxied out with safety announcements being drowned out with roars of 'Olé, olé, olé' and 'Oggy, oggy, oggy'. It all kicked off as passengers, spurred on by a lethal cocktail of drink and mass stupidity, caused a punch-up in mid-air that saw the captain return to their take-off point after a mere twenty-five minutes in the air.

'He just went to pieces,' one of the crowd tells me, referring to a mate who'd seen the uniforms and strict faces of United States' pre-clearance officials in Dublin and stayed at home. 'Bottled it,' he adds.

With so much time to burn and limited money to booze, I try and tell them about cheaper places than here, where a flat glass of beer comes over the counter if $8 makes its way to the other side. But they are having none of it: they've heard about an Irish pub across the road in the New York, New York Hotel and Casino. The Nine Fine Irishmen claims to be decades old, yet that'll do these lads. Perception. It's the typical Irish holiday of getting away to a place that's as close to home as possible.

Journalists who have covered previous bouts have plenty of stories to tell about the bandwagon and their endless adventures. One took a video of a group leaving the Floyd Mayweather weigh-in so hammered that the first out got on the wrong side of an escalator, and everyone else just followed. What ensued was a cross between calamity and comedy, with a crush barely averted as bodies capsized on top of bodies coming back up what they had presumed to be the downside, as knees were torn from new suits.

Those suits are a staple of the McGregor fan, of course: Three-piece and tweed.

Yet at times it's a new experience for some, clad in such predictability. One friend out here a few years ago for another manic McGregor episode walked into the bathroom after the open workouts to find a young lad from Dublin standing in the middle of the floor, panicking. 'I need to piss,' he kept saying, and when told he was already in the toilet, responded that his tailored trousers had a button as opposed to the zip he was used to. The alcohol was to blame for both his confusion, and for what inevitably came next.

It hasn't been that long since McGregor emerged, but it feels like it's gone on forever. Maybe it's him who has left us with a jaded sensation, like a middle-aged man who thinks he can still pull off an all-nighter. Or maybe it's his fans, who have been relentless.

For instance, it's only three years since around a thousand of them traipsed and fell into the heart of Dublin's financial district like the walking dead for a press conference with McGregor and Aldo. Questions from supporters were permitted, which turned the event into an absolute farce. Many of the queries made no sense; many more might have made sense had they only been intelligible. That would have been morning time stateside too, and further pushed the idea of the stereotypical Paddy: on the batter to the point of self-humiliation.

The idea much of MMA had liked to project up to that point was that, while there may have been violence, there was still dignity and respect. The Dublin press conference tore up that aspect. One prominent coach in Ireland even texted Aldo's coach afterwards to apologise, and there quickly was a clear distinction made between those who like the sport and those who like McGregor. Not once during that troglodytic episode did he attempt to place cream on the rash; instead he scratched at it, making it worse.

Unfortunately, due to McGregor's success and attitude, his entire journey has been a projection of new Irishness. His pseudo-nationalism has been selling Ireland in leprechaun-esque fashion with worn out and tattered lines like, 'They don't understand these crazy Irish men looking to take their head clean off. This is what we do; we've been doing it for generations,' and, 'If one of us goes to war, we all go to war.'

Such trite nothingness though is lapped up by those that cheer him on.

* * *

IF HIS FANS EMPOWER HIM, HE EMPOWERS THEM. IT'S a two-way model, each feeding off each other, creating a never-ending circle that allows for no introspection, let alone doubt.

It makes me want to scream out about what is in front of them but they cannot see. Besides, they'll shamelessly retort that he is merely in the Muhammad Ali tradition. What they fail to see with such comments is that he might be that, except stripped of the politics, of the originality, and force for greater good that defined Ali. In other words, and to be far more precise, McGregor is in the Ali tradition minus what made Ali so special.

This idea is overlooked through a lack of historical knowledge about the past and a lack of understanding regarding the present. Cassius Clay had wit. He was funny. So much so that he inspired too many imitators who'd play the trash-talking game but couldn't carry it off. Years on, fighters like McGregor are still at it, as the standard has continued to fall away. The difficulty of humour has been replaced by the ease of abuse.

Think back to the infamous 1974 episode of ABC's *Wide World Of Sports*. With Ali and Joe Frazier trying to whip up interest around their rematch, as if that was even needed, the former insulted the latter and was far too intelligent, to the point where Frazier erupted, unable to take it anymore. He didn't have the cerebral tools to fight back, so he literally fought instead. Howard Cosell described the contrast in the scuffle that followed. 'Ali is probably clowning, but there is no question that Joe Frazier is probably not clowning.'

After a much needed ad break, as they were separated and pulled off the studio floor, the show came back on air with an empty seat. Of course, it was Ali who had hung around. 'I would say there was anger on his part, Howard, but I'm not angry and still not angry. That's why I'm still here. The man shouldn't be that savage and illiterate to just jump up and stand over me. But I'm still not angry at him, because I don't think two black men should be on the television cussing and acting like savages. This man speaks ignorance.' He continued calmly with his point.

Contrast such an episode with the jibes of 'bitch' and 'you'll do nothing' that we hear now. Had McGregor been his opponent back then, you feel it would have been Frazier dominating the intellectual battle.

For those who disagree, ask yourself a question. Remember Ali showing up in Atlanta in 1996? Remember how lighting the Olympic torch felt like a moment to cling to? He was a monument to a time and a place, and years later, this was society paying belated respect to that. But no matter what happens in the coming days and no matter whether or not he beats Khabib, do you think if McGregor showed up in thirty years' time, people would feel the same? Will they honour him? Unlikely, as what he's transformed into is not honourable at all.

As another of the group of fans in the Park MGM pretends to go to the toilet and use it for its purpose, all the while rooting in his pocket for a bag of powder, I don't bother to ask them their thoughts, because the predictable answer would only frustrate me. But it dawns that there has to be more to these people and this phenomenon. I call Starn again to ask why, from his perspective as an anthropologist, there are so many people in awe of such shallowness.

'One thing with social media is fans have a sense of intimacy and connection with the athlete that they didn't have before,' he explains. 'Certainly, there's always been hero worship in human history and sports, all the way back to Babe Ruth and to Willie Mays. Before, it was putting your hero up on a pedestal. Now, there's a connection because we can follow them on Twitter, see their Instagram. There's a bond. It facilitates hero worship. It's as if these supporters think, "He's not just a hero but a person that I really know."

'Among other things, we are a more secular world, too. If you don't have a saint or god to worship and you are looking for someone, it's then the sports hero becomes the vehicle for hoax fantasies, desires, and identification. And there again is this back-and-forth mirroring of sport and society. We have so many stories of the fallen celebrity, the Tiger Woods who is on top of the world, who turns out to come from this fucked-up family scene, and the burden and expectation of fame didn't do him any good, either. There's a huge appetite, part of what interests us with our heroes is their ultimate downfall.

'But crucially, with McGregor, I feel this is about the moment as right now, in so many ways, the lid is off the pot of global culture. All this stuff that people were reluctant to say, or felt was too outrageous to say in public, is all over social media and everywhere else. And Conor McGregor is the perfect reflection of those large cultural changes.'

A man for a sad and sorry time and place, it seems. One in which we have traded heroes for ghosts.

Against that backdrop, what's another line of coke off the bathroom counter?

CHAPTER 4

PROPER TWELVE

WHEN THE BOY GETS LOST, AND THEREFORE GETS scared, the natural instinct is to run for home. Flight is always the go to, no matter how much they talk a damn good fight. Has Conor McGregor grown beyond the boy? Behind the caricature, is he still the boy?

The man in me will hide sometimes, to keep from being seen.

His home is here in the old outer city of Dublin, where he keeps popping up as he has again this January of 2019, perhaps lost and scared. His first house is a mere five-minute drive east of the Black Forge, his local pub, and ten minutes west from where some claim he's holed up in a house of ill repute in Dolphin's Barn.

It's the small, standard, semi-detached effort that lines the streets just a couple of rows back from the buses and relative bustle along the main road through Crumlin, although it's very different these days to what it was like when he lived here. With the cranes again playing an active part in the distant skyline, and the economy going so well for some, there's a huge shortage of houses, meaning people working in the capital have been pushed that bit further from the centre in the search of a place to bed down.

The prices have punched through the roof, and there is no sign of that ending. Dublin has been a base for major salaries around tech, banking, and pharmacy. One telltale result are those left behind via a massive social divide, as cardboard boxes and sleeping bags line curbs, human waste either replacing or residing with artificial waste.

For tourists on a return visit, many step over them and instead notice how the once wonderful old-man pubs in town have wine menus on the tables and are filled with kids fresh out of college on six-figure salaries paying crazy cash for en-vogue pale ales. It's due to get worse, with companies abandoning the UK around Brexit already eyeing up Dublin. What people in places like Crumlin notice, though, is the change in their community. The good times haven't affected their lives directly, but it's bringing in those they have affected. But what was it like when McGregor lived here in his youth?

The very nascent years, frankly, were normal.

He's spoken fleetingly to me in the past about it being a tough place, and how he'd had a rough time of it back then. 'The reason people take up combat sport is self-defence,' he explained. 'It's not just to get fit and make friends, they're a by-product of getting into combat sport. But young men go into this to be confident and know they can defend themselves in any situation.'

He was talking about personal experiences, more than any general trend. Indeed, some childhoods mean they can never really exist. While safer within the smaller confines and curfews of his earliest days, in McGregor's teenage years his boundaries widened and so did the scope for trouble. Of that, he has endless tales. He took a hiding over a girl one evening here, and a bad beating from a gang of ten another afternoon when his so-called friends ran for cover, all because it was wrongly alleged that he'd called someone a bottler. It got to the stage where he took the ends off a barbell, emptied the books from his school bag, and left the metal rod hanging out the top of it as a warning, in open view, as he strolled from class to class.

'I could give you another fifty stories of walking down the street and someone trying to start a fight,' he recalled when we last spoke. 'I don't know what it was, I was a quiet child. I know this sounds stupid, we were kids, but at the time you were petrified, and it played a part in the path I chose.' All in all, he was screaming without raising his voice.

Perhaps he still is.

Given that you can't jettison your past, you're left with two options. You can learn from it, or you can rage against it. For some time, it's option two that has been far more prevalent for McGregor. The outcome is the destruction of himself rather than the construction of a better self.

* * *

FOR THE MOST PART, NICE CARS SIT IN THE DRIVEWAYS of recently purchased houses, and a quick look in the windows of Crumlin's estate agents tells a story about the slow gentrification of this place. But there is another way to learn what it used to be like. Boxing clubs in such communities are like an incubator of the past: little ever changes.

The club in these parts is a stone's throw from the old McGregor residence. All those years ago, when he walked in, Phillip Sutcliffe and Stephen Kavanagh were there doing what they could to make sure a vital asset kept on keeping on. Today they still are, even if their wrinkles have increased from way back then and their tones are a bit more gravelly. Many talk about McGregor as a sporting hero, but these are the real sporting heroes.

I meander in and they put the kettle on, wash three cups resting in the sink, then sit down to talk about 'their kids' who came through the place and went out into the wider world. It's meant in more than a coaching way — as Kavanagh notes, 'It's like being a counsellor.' He's not wrong: boxing so often is a first, last, and only resort for many children born into working-class Ireland.

'It's very important. There are problems that were here long ago, like drink and drugs, but some kids today are also having an awful time around self-harming and suicide,' adds Sutcliffe. 'They all have their problems. My phone does be hopping here sometimes. Boxing clubs are underestimated in sport. Just look at government funding. They don't know what we do; we get very little from them. We survive on subs, donations, raffles.'

Sutcliffe boxed at the 1980 and 1984 Olympics, having won a handful of national titles and made the podium at a couple of European Championships. He then busted his hand, got into coaching, and re-opened this place in the early 1990s. Years later, they were still trying to turn a sow's ear into a silk purse, and it was then that they came across McGregor.

He was just shy of being a teenager at the time but reeked of one, and was loud and flash enough to make you wonder if it might be real rather than just a survival mechanism, given the bullying he says he endured.

With the duo having having hidden away in the club for the entirety of one weekend – laying new wooden floors, sanding them, and then varnishing them – come the Monday night a cocky lad came from the football pitch next door and trampled across it in boots covered in mud. 'Get them off ya,' were the first words roared at him upon entry to the fighting sphere.

Little acorns. Strange beginnings.

'His white football stockings, I remember it well,' recalls Kavanagh. 'So he walks up to the first bag there, and he starts thumping into it. "This is great, this is great, I want to join," he says. So we told him his parents had to sign him up, and his mother came in.'

'That's right,' interrupts Sutcliffe. 'Mags, the mother. She was in here with the sister, doing the yoga and the training. Wanted to lose a few pounds. A sound woman.'

'Anyway, that's how it started,' Kavanagh goes on. 'And he was a great buzzer in the club, not because of where he is now, but he'd come in full of energy. "What's the story, Phil? What's the story, Jack? What's the story, Steve?" He was one of them fellas. Always buzzing. There used to be a few photos on the wall of him from when he was young, but they were stroked. Some people came in with a screwdriver and that was them gone.'

'Enthusiastic,' continues Sutcliffe. 'Wasn't a bad boxer either. He's after achieving more than any of them money-wise, to be fair. Average boxer with a big wallop. A good whack. If he stayed at it, he could have been good, but he was coming and going, playing soccer, coming boxing. At fourteen and fifteen, he started the martial arts. So he was in between all sports. To make it here, you've to just do the one, but he always had that goal to do something. I never liked MMA, but he always trained that bit harder, always had a special persona.'

With the humility and hard work of their club, I ask what they make of him now, given so much of his personality rails against the notion of respect taught between these walls.

'I'd never seen that type of person; he'd always been a nice person, a decent auld skin,' responds Sutcliffe. 'He was never big headed. Well, he'd never go on with that show-business shite that he'd be doing since.

We don't take that in here, bragging and all that. He has to do that for publicity, I'd say. He's told how to get some sort of reaction.

'He'd send the odd text to me,' he adds. 'I asked him for a case of his Dublin 12 whiskey or whatever it's called, he didn't give it to me yet. He's never dropped in either, the shitebag. Not for money, but just to see the kids. He should come in and show his face.'

They did make a small few quid off him, mind, even if he never knew it. They rightly call the Mayweather fight a farce but still decided to screen it live in the club. It wasn't completely full, though, because Sutcliffe called it off the week before the bell. 'I didn't want trouble, and you could have got that. From anywhere around here. I'd know them all, because they probably all boxed here. It's okay in the daytime when you can talk to them sober and there's no bleedin' drugs in them. But night time, I wasn't having that. So I just pulled the plug and then quietly put it back on. That was a good thing that we did.'

Elsewhere, the more famous McGregor gets, the more of a mystery he becomes. The more we hear about him, the less we know about him. But it's interesting in these parts: you get a glimpse at some of the foundations. Too often, we focus on the what and the where at the end; too little do we scratch and ask about the how and the why as well. The former allows us to have a go at McGregor, but the latter is more complicated, because it offers explanations.

Sutcliffe's own son, who is now a pro boxer, would have sparred with McGregor back then. Jamie Kavanagh, another they coached all the way to the paid ranks, did so too. So did his uncle Paul Kavanagh, of whom there's a photo high on the wall, remembering a young man shot dead in his car by the Kinahan cartel in 2015 during the ongoing drug war. David Byrne grew up just a couple of doors down and would later be shot dead at the weigh-in for the WBO European lightweight title bout between Jamie Kavanagh and Antonio João Bento in the Regency Hotel across town. Byrne's brother Liam, reported as a

Kinahan member, would have hung around with McGregor, too.

It's a problem that's not spoken about but hinted at.

Indeed, you can gauge the situation by what's not said rather than what is. For sure, the bloody feud in these parts can be overstated, but it's probably better than understating it, with the reality somewhere between the red tops' and the *Irish Times'* take on it all.

Outside the doors of the club, talking about the Mayweather-McGregor night that was shelved before being put back on, one person offers to explain the situation on the condition they remain anonymous. 'You know all these people in the gangs through boxing; they are all big boxing fans. All that feud, it changed things in a big, big way around here. All these guys knew each other, grew up together, and they all live among each other. But there's money and greed, and you don't even want to be saying things, as certain people will quote you wrong, and then you'll get shot. It's like that. I know both sides and that's the problem. It's a small space.'

For many looking for something to talk about, some act to give out about, some misery to laugh about, this association between McGregor and certain shady characters suits. Quick and easy, they only want to see the ultimate collapse. Deeper and harder to understand, they never care much for the gradual decay.

They should.

Here in Crumlin there was the nature, but that's only ever half the story.

In that sense, what about McGregor and the nurturing that took place in his first home?

* * *

THESE DAYS, MCGREGOR'S FATHER TONY IS BETTER known as an amusement on Instagram. It's there he bemoans the amount of coinage given back to him by the ticket machine in the train station as he couldn't squeeze it in his Hugo Boss fitted suit. It's there he shows off the free Italian leather wallets sent his way in return for a marketing mention. It's there he's always aboard the 188, the boat bought for him by his son and named after the amount of social welfare Conor used to get when, he said, Tony was telling him to get a real job.

Once a taxi driver, you'd never guess as much.

Once against Conor's hopes, dreams, and wishes of making it in MMA, you'd never guess that either when he shows up ringside and lives well off of his son's successes. It's a demonstration of the moment when children become our parents and we revert to being children again.

If the greatest gift in life is someone believing in you, however, what *did* Tony give his boy?

In the past, Conor spoke briefly about the hardship, but since then, it's been the lack of words that have been most telling. One person close to him says he tried to delve into it a few times but never got anywhere. 'His childhood? It was either he found it difficult to remember things and he'd just say to talk to his folks and that might jog his memory, or he just flat out refused and didn't want to go there. Maybe there's something in that.'

If you talk to psychologists, they'll tell you that there's a lot to suggest that challenging relationships with parents will lead to some difficulty, more so in the case of extreme neglect or abuse. The way they understand problems is called formulation, and there are a lot of different ways to formulate. The most common and widely accepted one is called the five Ps: the factors are *problem, precipitating, perpetuating, protective,* and *predisposing.* It's the last on that list that this falls not so neatly into.

There have been shocking cases in sport like Aaron Hernandez. The

Boston Globe in 2018 released a podcast looking into what led the American football star to a life sentence for masterminding a murder followed by suicide in prison. It was predictably grim. We had for some time known about the degenerative brain condition CTE he endured, caused by too many hits to the head on game-day which took away part of his brain's ability to function normally and to reason. But there was far more to it. His brother Jonathan spoke of how gridiron meant everything to their father Terry, but Aaron wanted to be a cheerleader. That idea was removed quickly from his mind as 'it wasn't the definition of a man.' Instead, Terry pushed the sport, constantly used the slur 'faggot' around the house, and believed there was a masculine and feminine way to stand, to look, to place your hands. 'The person you look up to is your father, that's your king,' Jonathan said.

Cause and effect.

That was off the scale, but if there are two questions I could ever ask McGregor and be guaranteed an honest, in-depth answer, it would be the following. Firstly, what would he change? Secondly, what was his relationship like with *his* king before fame and fortune? They may provide the same answer. They may tell us a lot about the route recently taken. At the very least, they would give you a sense of what lies behind the curtain. We may never know.

Back inside the boxing club, Sutcliffe talks about a recent split among the group of friends. 'They all knew each other and all supported him. My own young fella went to Vegas. Jamie too. They never lost that contact, but a lot of the people after this …, they are staying away from Conor a bit. I don't care what anyone says, money changes everyone. Some for good, some for bad. But it changes everyone.

'He needs to get his act together,' he adds coldly.

He's right, of course. Except for the fact that needing, wanting, and being able to do something are very different matters. Especially when this is the home to which the boy takes flight.

Storm clouds are raging all around my door, I think to myself, 'I might not make it any more.'

CHAPTER 5

DUMB, GETTING DUMBER

OCTOBER 2018 TIPTOES TO THE DOORSTEP, AND IT quickly becomes clear why most Americans who come to Las Vegas only ever do so for a couple of nights. Already ten days in town and with the soul destroyed, this place next goes after the body. Coming in one night, a receptionist asks if there's anything I need. I suggest she take my shoe laces and belt before I go to my room, just to be safe. In the robotic world of their service industry, sarcasm and humour fail miserably.

'We can do that for you, sir. That's no problem.'

While not unexpected, the reply does come as one more disappointment. It's a reminder that I could answer a basic how-are-you-today query with a detailed yarn about how my entire family had just been wiped out in a horrific car crash and the response would be, 'That's great, sir.' Her perfect white teeth and spray-on smile only make the empty feeling worse, so belt and shoe laces are accompanied to my room by six beers.

Anything to dull the pain.

Most mornings are greeted with a half-full can sitting on the nightstand, the warm smell a sickly souvenir of the night before. The television shows me nauseating warnings of the day ahead and the level that awaits outside under the bright, burning desert sun. There's a stream of similarly themed ads about skipping queues for liver transplants, suing chemical companies, getting a pay-out for hair loss after chemotherapy. They all share the notion of selling people a way to con a system which they lack the intelligence to thrive in. A system about the status quo.

What does this have to do with Conor McGregor, you might rightly ask. Well, he is nothing in terms of status, fame, and wealth without society laughing at his quips, lusting after his form, and indulging his attitude. And this is an insight into that society.

There are those who call McGregor a marketing genius for the sell, but when these are examples of the level of buyer, is it that impressive? Many years ago, on *The Late Late Show*, Ireland's heavyweight Friday night chat effort, Richard Dawkins popped up and had an audience member ask him about where evolution would take us next. Awaiting a response about the possibilities that lay ahead, he was disappointed to be informed that we are very much in a phase of devolution, a slump from which we might never recover, like an airplane in free fall after its tail has been clipped.

The audience of *The Late Late Show* is a microcosm of this, too. The programme used to look at social issues in a land once oppressed by everyone from the British, to the church, to the country's politicians and elites. If it had its finger on the pulse back then, maybe it still does now, when it's watched by a middle-class crowd sitting in lazy ignorance, looking for the lowest form of entertainment in so many ways.

McGregor had been on the show the week before we met in 2013, and looking back it is telling viewing, given where the narrative pushed the conversation and ultimately him. 'If Muhammad Ali was from Dublin, he'd sound like you,' proclaimed host Ryan Tubridy, though there was little evidence on show from his guest to back up such a statement. Still, it wouldn't be a last time that such a comparison was made.

Given that McGregor had yet to develop his Notorious persona, Tubridy could have taken the interview down many interesting paths, from classism to psychology, from philosophy to dreams. He chose not to.

A few months on, he was back, and it was as if that last comment set the tone. What McGregor was doing was working in the eyes of those in the studio, so he continued on with the effort. This time, his introduction after back-to-back UFC wins was as 'one of the most exciting and charismatic Irish sporting figures'. And it rapidly descended from there.

McGregor: I'm main-eventing this time.

Tubridy: The moment I met you the last time, I said, 'This is going to be the beginning of a long relationship between you and me on this show.'

McGregor: I'm like the male version of Sinéad O'Connor, on every week.

Tubridy: In a manner of speaking. And also you make me feel like a tramp, you're so well dressed, as always.

Tubridy addresses McGregor's most recent UFC victory, over Max Holloway in the States.

McGregor: It [the last fight] went exactly like I said. I said I was going to go in and whoop his ass, and I went in and whooped his ass.

He continues on the theme later on in the interview when asked whether fame or money motivates him.

McGregor: Fame does not motivate me. What motivates me is human movement and money. That's it. If it doesn't involve either of them, I'm going to roll over and have another hour's sleep.

Tubridy: That's brilliant. I'm speechless. It's so entertaining ...

The interview perhaps inevitably moves on the subject of celebrity, his 'new mate' Arnold Schwarzenegger and a photo with P. Diddy.

McGregor: P. Diddy's a little up his own ass, to be honest.

Tubridy: Oh, that's great.

By then, association with his burgeoning fame was such that come 2014, McGregor received yet another invitation, the third dot lining up with the trajectory of the first two.

One exchange during that interview, on the subject of McGregor's next opponent, Cole Miller [who would later pull out due to injury], went as follows:

McGregor: He's a tall American, he's experienced, he's been around the game a long time. [Looking at a photo] There he is, he's not the best looking guy. I wanted a better looking opponent. It is what it is. He called me out.

Tubridy: Why did you want a better looking opponent?

McGregor: He's an ugly ... He's an experienced guy, he's been around the game a long time. He's fought under the UFC banner sixteen or seventeen times, he's been around the game a long time. He opened his mouth and said I was a show pony. He said I was this, he said I was that.

Tubridy: Let's get the quotes right, because first of all, you called him a lanky twat and a jobber. What's a jobber?

McGregor: A jobber is a guy that they keep around that's not that good, but they bring him in to make the good guys look even better. He's a jobber, He's showing up in Dublin to get his ass whooped and make me look really good in my home town.

Tubridy: He said about you, he said your jaw is going to be so weak from running your mouth off that he's going to take you out in the first round.

McGregor: Yeah, this is good. Like I said, he's been around the game. It's going to be a different feel when he steps in that octagon in the O2 [Arena]. I'm someone he's never faced before. He thinks there's a lot of pressure on me because it's in my home town. There's a lot of pressure on him. A lot of the guys in the division aren't happy with the way I've been speaking and the attention I've been getting. He's the guy that's stepping forward to answer questions for these other guys. There's a lot on his back, but he's not the man to answer the question. I'm looking forward to seven weeks' time; I'm going to shut his mouth.

There's laughter and applause.

Tubridy: He said of you that you're just a mental midget who shoots his mouth off. He said, 'I want to hurt him.' Is he gonna hurt you?

There's more laughter.

McGregor: No, he's not going to lay one finger on me Ryan. I love this, this creates drama. Drama creates emotion, and emotion creates dollars at the end of the day. He's going to come in, there's hype. He's said a lot, I've said a lot. Now we get the show on. A lot of people are going to tune in out of curiosity. 'Who's this loud-mouth Irish guy that keeps talking all this shit about everyone?' Now here's the time I'm going to prove what I've been talking.

Tubridy: What are you going to do to this guy?

McGregor: I believe in my preparation. I believe my movement is too dynamic. I believe I'm going to freeze him with my movement and put him away.

Tubridy: Do you think it's going to take you long?

McGregor: I don't see it going beyond the first round, to be honest. He's going to approach me and try and make the fight ugly. But as you can see sitting here next to me, Ryan, I'm just too damn pretty.

There's uproarious laughter and another, louder burst of applause.

This was what was chalked down as interesting and amusing in this era. This is what we crawl after, the level of banter we crave, begging for some more.

Those being paid for providing this are giving a dunce populous what they want, not what they need. Tubridy provides the platform, McGregor obliges, the crowd follows.

The shallower the brook, the more it babbles.

* * *

IT'S A SORRY ROAD THAT'S BEEN TRAVELLED SINCE those early days in the public glare, but for McGregor and his defenders it again comes back to profit justifying all. Forbes reckon he will have brought in around $100m in 2018 to add to so much more and, if that says much about him, then it says much about the public. Feed the system and it will feed you.

With McGregor, we were given this piece of Play-Doh to mould and shape into what we wanted. It's long become clear that he would be whatever we chose as long as we were willing to pay. And this is what we came up with? A guy who engages in xenophobia and racism, spits bile, hurls bottles, and treats many with and against him with utter contempt.

Consider his press conference leading up to this Nurmagomedov fight from only last month in New York. Take in the extracts, as they are what inspire those who follow him as a god.

'If I was an owner and was part of the promotion, I would have had the fucking fans in this arena. Where's the fucking fans at? That's who pays the fucking bills. That's who deserves this show. Bring me all over the fucking world, and we're just sitting here in a fucking thing. I'm on probation and up to me eyeballs in ongoing and incoming civil cases. And we come here to do this bullshit. Here we are. You wanted a war, you know what I'm saying? Let's get a war going. Fuck all this stupid other shit.'

That wasn't all.

'I came back for the love of this, to come and shut this man up. A little rat, a little weasel, a little hard man in groups. I've met many of them through my years, a man who grows up in numbers, but on his own and when confronted in a similar situation cowers away and that's what you saw on the bus with that little sh*te over there. He sh*t his jocks after doing something to his own countryman that had nothing got to do with anything. That's it, I came back for the love of fighting and the love of war. I am going to truly, truly love putting a bad, bad beating on this little glass-jaw rat.'

And ...

'Fanboy. The man was a fanboy. He bought t-shirts of mine. He f*cking supported the cause. Do you remember that, you little fanboy? You little fanboy b*tch. He bought t-shirts to support the cause, nothing but respect.'

And ...

'Mamamamama, shut your mouth mate. You're a dirt box. You're absolutely dirt. Your last fight was embarrassing. We were laughing in the Brooklyn lock-up. We were laughing in a cell in Brooklyn at ya. Shite boy.'

A combination of thuggery and idiocy passing for diversion and satisfaction.

One of the journalists at that gig — at least he got in with press accreditation — even got the mic and talked about how he drank McGregor's whiskey until four in the morning at an Irish bar. What wasn't mentioned was that he probably killed more brain cells listening to his idol's nonsense than via any amount of heavy boozing. Still, as long as McGregor knows this, and even for a brief second acknowledges it.

David Marshall, a research professor and chair of new media, communication, and cultural studies at Melbourne's Deakin University, has spent years studying the effects of this current culture on how we view and present ourselves. I put in a call to him. 'We have an unstable sense of what defines boundaries, and we're constantly in a game in itself of producing and talking about those boundaries,' he explains. 'I've developed over the last decade this idea of persona studies as emerging from celebrity culture, but we are all engaged in some mediatised public version of ourselves. Before, the closest thing to it was us walking on the street and determining what we wore each day. But now, we kind of curate ourselves. This is where the modern chaos and confusion is. We have a very unstable culture that is hugely unpredictable around the formations of what we'll see in politics, the organisation of our entertainment, and forms of pleasure, as it's such a major shift in how we imagine ourselves individually and collectively. That is gigantic.'

According to Marshall, what is happening now is similar to the changes that took place 300 to 400 years ago. Basically, we are seeing a shift in the notion of what it is to be human at a larger level, and McGregor and others are playing with and preying off this. 'For most of the intervening period, we've had the model of an individual brain,' he says. 'However, that is beginning to break down. There is something different now via this network culture that is producing a different relationship. A collective brain in a cognitive sense. Constantly, we are trying to work out how we connect. So, the idea of author and authority is shifting in this new collective world, and we may not have the same relationship to the individual and to the social. And in terms of the research around it, there are major changes in the formation of celebrity that are based on aspects of social media. So, you have a different constellation of ranges of celebrity that may or may not be organised the way the entertainment industry has done it for a century or more.

'In Asia, they call them KOLs — Key Opinion Leaders. "Influencers" is another term that's used. So, we have a lot of what can't be described as a public as we understood for a long time. I call them micro-publics: even though there might be millions of people, they are millions of people I might not know are attached to an individual. I see this with my children. They might have relationships to Taylor Swift that I don't know about. The relationship is odd in the sense they are following them on Instagram which isn't that different to magazines thirty years ago, but the difference is they don't share that with anyone else that isn't following Taylor Swift. Therefore, we are developing publics that aren't publics. I don't know what my children listen to in music, what they follow really in sport, I don't really know where their interests lie. They are teens, nearly adults. And that's pretty much pandemic. I'd say we have a different sense of connection — emotional, time, sentiment — that is difficult to say how that is connected to others.'

He alludes to his own eldest son, 21, who he is aware has an interest in McGregor, but he has no real knowledge beyond that as his son doesn't need to share that. Instead, he can text about it in his own circle of people. There, no matter what McGregor does or says, it's accepted as the new normal and from there he can push boundaries again while always receiving praise. As for the fans, it means they only listen to those they agree with. This has big impacts around the notion of the truth and false claims and how celebrities can behave. Some talk about how we think more but hear the same thing over and over, and that's really true.

All of this affects the celebrity in new ways, as well as what we consider to be a celebrity. McGregor is both an influencer of this new world and a sporting guinea pig for this new world.

'This is where our echo chamber of knowledge is too specialised,' Marshall suggests. 'We almost need a massive interdisciplinary reading of this, so it's not just neuropsychologists and neurologists. We need people who are reading what's happening to high school students, people who understand what is really their inattention economy, as opposed to attention economy. A close attachment to something that breaks within fifteen seconds. We need a lot of research to get there.'

* * *

THIS IS THE WORLD PEOPLE LIKE MCGREGOR THRIVE IN.

Just take his own social media image that is worth so much to him.

Everything there is either an addition to the illusion, yet another demonstration of his wealth, or, more recently, an endless marketing campaign: people are sending in pictures of themselves drinking his brand of whiskey in the hope of getting an acknowledgement and a retweet. Seven-and-a-half million now find this intriguing enough to follow on Twitter. 32 million follow him on Instagram. Another 7.8 million do so on Facebook. At best, McGregor might recognise their existence; at worst, they get to look at him sitting topless on a car bonnet or in a new suit or on a private jet.

In one sense, it's nothing new.

The author Ray Bradbury saw it coming as early as 1953 via his book *Fahrenheit 451*. In it, during the advent of television, the wife, Mildred, is obsessed with media to the point that she stays in her parlour all the time, where three of the walls are screens. She wants to make the fourth the same so she may be completely surrounded and absorbed by a reality drama she watches non-stop and of which she herself is a part.

'Social media is taking this further forward, and the key is you are involved, or at least the trick is you *think* you are involved,' says Mark Bauerlin, a professor of English at Emory University in Georgia and author of *The Dumbest Generation: How the Digital Age Stupefies Young*

Americans and Jeopardizes Our Future. 'And that is the interactive audience involvement we see now. It's addictive and makes people feel closer to their hero, be that McGregor or whoever. People are participating in media, and it's a kind of drug under the guise of activity. So, you're not just a passive receiver; you're actually part of what's happening, which is of course a great, big lie.'

When the chemical industry was dumping waste with impunity and still managing to increase its value, eventually there had to be, and was, a conversation around the cost to everyone else. With social media, that conversation is not being had. Steve Jobs once talked about technology and the idea of bicycles for the mind and enthused about its ability to empower people. But while the products may be okay at heart, the business model exploits that and exploits everyone. Investors love it for the returns, but they are getting those returns off the back of societal decline. McGregor is part of that.

Take Silicon Valley. Once the pride of the world, it now ought to be treated with disdain. Only it's not, despite and because of the dumbification it's aiding and abetting.

'We have hugely sped up the decline through mass communication,' Bauerlein adds. 'Everyone has a voice, an opinion; everyone deserves to be heard. This is the ethos. The social media design, you should be able to share everything and tell everything about yourself. It's a great big flattery game they play, and you can always find someone to reinforce. Some opinions shouldn't be reinforced, and just look at Conor McGregor for that. You shouldn't feel certain things. You will always find someone to back you up though, and share in your idiocy. There's a lot of them out there. And what you have is all these guys insulting one another, saying things you'd never ever say to a person's face. Or if you did, you better have your guard up.'

McGregor's fans are all too willing to back anything their hero says up, and they think copying his persona gives them a free pass. They love that about him and what it offers up as acceptable.

It's a sorry situation, and to exist it takes a level of acceptance rather than questioning, a level of ignorance rather than understanding.

* * *

HERE IN VEGAS, A LOOK AROUND THE RESTAURANT

at lunch offers another reminder that this all plays into and amounts to the new way. Dumb getting dumber. One woman comes in from the pool and calls over the waitress who brought her the drink she's clasping. She's not happy. She claims the ice shouldn't be crushed; meanwhile, an offer of a new one doesn't stop her in her tracks. She's a wrecking ball. Her basic request quickly comes with a life story.

'I know this because I used to work in a bar, you know. You might not think that to look at me now, but I wasn't always 250 pounds. I used to be skinny, but then my mother got sick and I had to move to Chicago and I got a job in an insurance office, and it all changed ...'

Drink replaced, next she comes over to me and starts talking about how the previous drink had crushed ice, but she knows that shouldn't be the case because she used to work in a bar. I feign interest and, upon hearing my accent, she starts talking about McGregor.

'I love that guy.'

Of course she does.

'He's so funny.'

Of course he is.

'He's so clever.'

Of course he is.

'He's so rich.'

Of course he is.

Finally, she leaves.

Still, her voice can be heard carrying from the other side of the room. She's cornered another poor soul, and he's not getting out of this any time soon.

'I wasn't always 250 pounds. I used to be skinny, but then my mother got sick and I had to move to Chicago, and I got a job in an insurance office, and it all changed ...'

CHAPTER 6

COACH

THE HEAD OF GOD IS SHORN.

The face of God is pockmarked by red zits.

The voice of God is unsure at times as he talks to an interviewer through a beat-up mic.

Here in Dublin, 2019 passes on by but the harsh and tedious weather doesn't.

Sitting in from the wind and rain, I'm looking at a video of a very different Conor McGregor.

A scared little boy at times. A fusion of wonder and fear.

The year is 2008, and he is being asked to compare the life he is now living, training full-time for the first time, to the life he has just left, the nine-to-five job as an apprentice plumber he held down before walking out on his employer. He gets confused, says it is a difficult question, and doesn't emerge with any actual answer.

Then it gets back to the two interwoven strands God likes talking about.

MMA. And himself.

'I'm an up-and-coming fighter and without a doubt, you'll see me in the UFC in the near future,' he says. 'It's an addiction, it's all I do, I don't think about anything else. It's as simple as that,' he says. 'I was a plumber, an apprentice plumber, I did a year in that and it just wasn't for me. It's all or nothing in the game I'm in. I felt I had enough talent and dedication and love for the sport to give it my all,' he says. 'My dream is to be world lightweight champion in the UFC, have more money than I know what to do with, have a great life for my kids and my grandkids, everyone in my family,' he says. 'Words can't even describe what it would mean to fight in UFC. It's where I want to be. I'm a hundred percent confident. I have the skills and dedication, and it's what I really want,' he says.

It's strange how our cynicism strips away the dream and hurriedly puts a dreamer down, like it's holding the looking glass up to our own cowardice while we queue up as told.

It would be another five years before McGregor made his UFC debut and, at the time, the ghetto lifestyle he now sells so profitably and easily, and lives so destructively, had been ripped from under him. Back in 2005, when he was sixteen, his parents had got together the money to purchase a bigger house in the comparatively leafy Dublin suburb of Lucan.

'The back arse of nowhere,' McGregor said about his new digs. 'I certainly did not handle it well,' he added. 'I eventually did. But at the time, I had a lot of resentment towards my family. I was really upset for a long time after that.'

It meant Crumlin Boxing Club was too far. As was his school, so he went to the Gaelscoil, or Irish-speaking school, Coláiste Cois Life. It wasn't just the language that was different. Though torn from so much of what he knew, he found what he loved through a new classmate, Tom Egan.

Across those mid-2000s, each morning before class, he and Egan would chatter, reliving MMA bouts they'd watched over the weekend. When passion meets inspiration, obsession is born.

McGregor had tried to add kickboxing to his skill set of flailing fists; Egan was studying Brazilian jiu-jitsu as a lowly white belt. One weekend, the former suggested coming over to stay in the latter's house, and they ended up retreating to a cramped shed for hours. It was there they started to practice what they didn't really know yet. They grew together.

Indeed, by 2006, Egan had introduced McGregor to his future coach, John Kavanagh.

Not long after, Egan also mentioned he had a friend who worked for Irish sports TV channel Setanta, and through him, the two of them somehow got tickets for UFC 75. Both headed to London to witness a card featuring Matt Hamill and Michael Bisping, and Dan Henderson and Quinton Jackson, and to witness a future no one thought they'd ever truly have.

'It was my first time seeing all the celebrity fighters, the president Dana, I was blown away,' McGregor told me back in 2013. 'Bruce Buffer, the announcer, was there. I said, "Will you say my name?" "Now entering the octagon," he roared, "Colin," and he trailed off. Even [to] the referee, a famous one, I said, "You'll be rescuing guys from me one day." I was a kid, loving all of it.'

It had a huge impact, as if the last little push he needed to make sure it was his life. McGregor came home and put up clips of knockouts on his Bebo account, typing underneath, 'Check this UFC out, my future job ... Please God'.

The responses varied from cruel to mocking, but he didn't care.

He started working that aforementioned job, but for someone with his drive and charisma that was never going to do. Soon, he walked out on it and began going to the gym twice a day.

This is the backstory the fans love because it's accessible.

This is the backstory the media love because it's inspirational.

This is the backstory the UFC love because it's profitable.

But you don't buy a house simply by looking at the outside. Instead, you step inside.

I contact Egan, who himself made it as far as the UFC for just one night, looking to talk about the past. His response reads: 'I don't want anything to do with Conor McGregor. He's extremely selfish and disrespectful. Sorry.' I try again given the piece of the puzzle he is.

'Don't take this personal, it's just I don't want to contribute to someone who doesn't contribute to anything in any form, and that's including friendship. And I was home recently but [that] was just for the family. If you're ever in Boston I'd grab a pint with you.'

Remember, when there's a then, there's a now.

Looking for answers merely throws up yet more questions.

The common conundrum of Conor.

* * *

THERE IS ANOTHER WAY TO SEE PAST A DOOR THAT has been bolted.

John Kavanagh was like a father figure for McGregor in those times.

In 2016, he sat down with Paul Kimmage, perhaps the best Irish sports interviewer of all. A former pro cyclist himself who, in his second career as a journalist, helped bring down Lance Armstrong, initially Kimmage had turned up to talk with McGregor, but when the subject didn't show, the coach took his place.

This has become a theme, with Kavanagh often trying to interject in order to save McGregor from himself. He tells other journalists more and more lately that his fighter will only talk to someone of the stature of Canadian MMA journalist Ariel Helwani. Then he tells Helwani that McGregor will only talk to The Mac Life, his own website. On it goes.

The little Dutch boy saving Haarlem by putting his finger in the dike.

Kavanagh recalled McGregor's first day at Straight Blast Gym, which was fascinating for a whole variety of reasons on a whole variety of levels. Owen Roddy, who is now his striking coach, was the best they had and was supposed to spar the new kid. But the new kid wanted to fight. As an introduction, he caught Roddy with a shot to the jaw and dropped him. Aisling Daly was another star, and she was next in his way. McGregor threw a body shot that landed on the sweet spot and put her on the canvas.

'I got a little emotional because Ash had been with me a long time and the other guys would look after her,' Kavanagh remembered. 'But this new guy had come in and put her down, and my protective nature kicked in. I was still fighting at that stage, or hadn't stopped that long, so I put the gloves on ... Actually, Conor has corrected me on that and says it was bare knuckles. But anyway, I held him down and beat the shit out of him, without putting too fine a point on it. I kept hitting him in the body until he couldn't breathe, and then I looked at him. "What's it going to be? We can train or we can fight."'

The next day, McGregor showed up again, and it got a bit better from there.

He listened, learned, took in a few things. Improved in both mind and body. And eventually worked his way up to a fight. 'My first fight?' he said to me. 'A dingy hall, in a boxing ring. I was supposed to be the first fight, so I showed up twenty minutes before. On a boxing bill, that's how we did it. It was laid back. I approached the MMA similar, but John Kavanagh ran over. "You're late, you've to get medicals done."

'They moved me from first fight to the third fight to make time, threw me in the back, got the medicals, and threw me in the ring. It didn't register until I was standing across from this big, tough Nordie, and I thought, "What the fuck have I got myself into?" I was barefoot, [with] tiny gloves that barely covered the knuckles, bare shins, no head guard. I was in a pair of surf-dude shorts that a friend had left in my suitcase after a holiday.'

Gary Morris wasn't from Northern Ireland as it turns out, but memory skews minutiae. McGregor's first fight has been reduced to a footnote by both time and the scale of what he's achieved since. Morris was actually a Dubliner too, and lasted until eight seconds out from the end of round two. 'I don't know what you want to know,' he says when I interview him about McGregor. 'We were two kids having a fight, that was all.' Morris moved on. McGregor soon moved onto a first defeat.

'I used to run these little shows in Good Counsel [GAA club] down the road, and I'd give the guys tickets to sell and give them a commission or whatever,' added Kavanagh. 'So Conor had a bunch of tickets, all his mates were there, and he was the name, the rising star. He was fighting this skinny little Lithuanian fella who just ran through him. I keep saying it, fighters don't mind getting hurt but hate being embarrassed. That was an embarrassment for him.'

The Lithuanian was Artemij Sitenkov. He was both skinny and little. Those close to his camp recall that evening back in 2008 and insist that Kavanagh wanted to make sure 'the name' became a bigger name. They claim he wanted a small opponent and allege he used a different set of scales at the weigh-in to make it look legit, although the truth is lost to the past.

The outcome isn't.

In the build-up and with friends in Ireland, they told Sitenkov of his opponent's attitude. At nineteen, McGregor was not only claiming that he'd win but that it would be a knockout of a guy with six more fights under his belt. 'When an opponent doesn't expect anything serious from you, you have a little advantage,' Sitenkov says. 'Conor was way too confident. Young, the rising star, too much belief in himself. We were talking a lot before the fight. He was trying to scare with his looks, his words. Looking into my eyes like a beast. It's usual behaviour for a newcomer, and I knew it. Of course, it evolved in terms of him since then. He's more provocative now and more dangerous too, as perhaps he started to believe the crazy. But then, it was funny to see a nineteen-year-old trying to scare you with a look. I'd been around too long.'

As for the fight itself, it was almost as easy to trick youth out on the canvas. McGregor wanted to throw punches so Sitenkov would drop his hands and pretend it was to be a boxing match. But there wasn't a strike landed before the Lithuanian dived in and won on the ground with a kneebar submission. 'After the fight, we had several conversations. I lived in Ireland for a year, we met several times. He was a pretty decent, simple guy. "How are you, how's your training?" A regular guy without any arrogance or envy. So maybe there was a lesson as he went away, found new motivation, came back better.'

It's weird the way the world works: Sitenkov would go on to become number one in Europe in his weight class but failed to make the UFC for economic reasons. According to him, UFC had no interest in the eastern half of the continent in terms of shows or gyms, so they didn't need any locals. It did, however, very nearly end McGregor's career — and not just because of the result.

'All my friends and family heard I was doing this crazy thing where you can kick and wrestle and all this mad stuff,' he has explained to me of that night. 'Then I go out and lose, submission. "Fuck this crap," I thought. I just drifted away. Nearly gave up on it all.'

There was more than the shame of defeat, though. There was the shame of stealing. 'I was only a kid, and people were handing me €30 for a ticket. I'd go to the shop, dip into it. Then sell another ticket. Over the course of six weeks, €600 was gone. I didn't have anything to pay John with … I don't know where this is going, it's going weird now,' he continued, as if his past was trying to drag him back down with it.

'Look, I spent all the money, lost that fight, legged it, didn't answer my phone to him because he was looking for the money. I just disappeared. These kind of things happened a couple of times. But through all of that, John kept taking me back in. I don't like even thinking or talking about all that, because them days are over. They are gone. They are done with.'

After the money went missing, Kavanagh decided he didn't mind the thief going missing as well. Then McGregor's mother called him. 'It was one of the first times, maybe the first time, that a parent had reached out to me,' Kavanagh said. 'It got me thinking. "Maybe I have a bigger role here than punching and kicking. Maybe I'm doing a bit more for them than I thought." I guess I started to realise that a lot of people get into fighting for the same reasons I did — it's not for the fighting; they are dealing with something in their childhood. And I wasn't going to turn my back on someone in trouble. But I thought it was a waste of time, and my best friend at that time, Dave Roche, he thought it was a waste of time. Conor is a bit of a street kid. Dave felt he'd fall off the wagon or go back down the same pathway in a couple of months.

'But I had to give it a shot.'

In the end, he called to his house. 'I was used to this bubbly, charismatic athlete, but he looked very down and just didn't look healthy to me,' Kavanagh said. 'So we had a conversation that I've had with a couple of guys since. "You don't want to be the guy in your forties saying coulda, shoulda, woulda with a pint in your hand at the bar. You've got potential. Use it. Do it. Don't worry about the ticket money. Scratch it off, I don't care." He didn't say much. He was mostly listening. It sounds silly, but it was kind of emotional.

'He started crying — and I'll cry watching *Free Willy*, that's just my nature. But I felt he was going to give everything to me. Maybe we hadn't been the best of friends up to this point, and we certainly weren't the best of friends when he ran off with the money as it was a lot, but I felt he was going to give everything to me. That was going to be a clean start.'

There are fine lines between falling and fortune.

Not that it was easy thereafter. It rarely was, although details are thin. To put it as Richard Ford did in his glorious book *The Sportswriter*, 'My own history I think of as a postcard with changing scenes on one side but no particular or memorable messages on the back.'

For McGregor, those changing scenes were the makings of the man we see now.

For instance, there's a theory that the nickname Notorious, and therefore the origins of the brand, came much later along with the lights, cameras and action. This simply isn't true. Those close to this will tell you it came from Kavanagh back then and was based on his out-of-octagon exploits rather than anything he did inside of the cage. He was basically trouble and what that was depends on who you talk to. A day in Drimnagh and there is chatter that by the time he was twenty he was an enforcer. 'There's loads of stories of him pucking the teeth out of this guy and that because people owed money,' says a person. This cannot be verified. Another says that shortly after, he'd gone up the food chain and had some enforcers of his own. This cannot be verified. It all adds to the myths around the man.

Sleeping dogs haven't been so much as let lie in this case, they've been put down.

But what is evident is that whatever he was up to at that point, he was professional only in name for there's no way he was fully committed to what would later become his religion. Right up to that defeat, and on to a November 2010 loss to Joseph Duffy that meant he'd lost 33 percent of his first six fights, he was one-dimensional. What he brought into the cage – as Sitenkov attested to – were the boxing basics that he'd picked up in the Crumlin club.

Of course, if you're going to have only one real quality in MMA then this is the one to have, as with both fighters starting out on their feet, you get the chance to throw a punch before anyone can take you down. Indeed those same boxing skills, albeit it heavier and honed, later took him to the top of UFC and towards the top of sports, showing that for all the complications and diversity, a good right or left hand gives you a huge chance of going far in this game. However, when the fists failed it was curtains.

If that's all he had in attack, his defense showed the same problems. Those two defeats came by way of submission. But there was a juncture where he finally decided to get serious, where he started to get into the ground game, where he began his trek to the very top of Cage Warriors.

It can seem small-time now, if only because of where he went, but his efforts there shouldn't be overlooked. Back in the late 2000s and across the turn of the decade, it was a relatively big deal. Bellator hadn't evolved to its Europa League level next to the UFC's Champions League status, so this was a serious stepping stone. And McGregor was bounding across the rocks with a pomp, quickly getting noticed not just for his persona but also for his genuine ability, which was growing. His rise within that realm with quite meteoric. He started detonating his left hand in each fight, as those across from him tended to be incapable of living with his power. All seemed to be going to plan.

Yet despite his ascent to two-weight world champion within that

Cage Warriors promotion, he was still living off social welfare. He couldn't so much as get a sponsor to have the costs of a tub of his protein covered. He was making steps forward, only to be hauled back by the reality of his standing in a niche sport.

For half a decade, from his debut in 2008 until his big break and bigger breakthrough, his annual income from MMA was coming in at around €1,500. UFC remained a no go, despite his promises to himself on camera. Doubts began to emerge, eating away at him for a while.

Something else took its place in that void.

* * *

LIKE SOME UNIQUE CHARACTERS BEFORE HIM, what makes McGregor so dangerous to himself out of the octagon has often made him dangerous to others in it. When comedian and UFC commentator Joe Rogan sat across from actor Jamie Foxx for an edition of his podcast in 2017, the subject of Mike Tyson and personality came up. 'You have to have it,' Foxx explained. 'Like back in the day, Mike was a wild boy. To hang out with him, you could understand he was the biggest person on the planet and he had demons. But he was fun, too. You see him in a club and he sees some girls, and he was like, "Fine, how you doing, do you like BMWs? You like cars, you like BMWs?" He'd take the girls out and go get a BMW, he was that crazy. He'd open up the dealership. But like I was saying, you can't have that type of talent in one area and ... You can't drink milk and nearly kill someone. Look at Hendrix, look at Elvis, they have to have some deficiency, because that's God fucking with us. He gives you something incredible, but he's also going to give you something to anchor that. Yin and yang.'

That's not to put McGregor on that level, because his results and his status simply do not match up, and it's not to defend him either. But it is to look into a sort of madness that can get you to the top of your sphere, a place that only inspires much more madness.

Where, then, did the climb begin?

Well, it's seven years since he won his first belt via Cage Warriors Featherweight Championship.

That was the end of the beginning, rather than the beginning of the end.

It was 2 June 2012 when he fought the busy, tough and smart Dave Hill for that crown. The Englishman had only lost two of his twelve fights, had never been stopped and was seen by experts as seriously durable, but he had never come across anything like this. These days Hill is retired, and while so many fighters are either scared to talk openly about experiences as if a sign of weakness, let alone admit to actual weakness, he's refreshingly different. 'I hadn't heard of him,' he recalls of the build-up. 'Well, I say that. I'd kind of heard his name once or twice, but I'd never seen his fights or anything like that. My coach at the time, Marc Goddard, he said, "You're matched with this guy Conor. Give him a look, you are fighting him in Ireland in a couple of months." I had a look through his fights and could see he was pretty handy and lairy.'

Once it was announced, the baiting began instantly, just as it had with Sitenkov.

But it was no longer a shield for McGregor.

The void had been filled as it had consumed him and had become a weapon.

Hill remembers going on social media and being met with a steady drip of comments from McGregor's mates, telling him he was going to get hurt, how he didn't stand a chance, that he'd soon be battered. He'd been around, but this was off the charts. 'Usually, it was always quite amicable before fights. But then, the week before, there was a radio interview to promote it. We were both on, and he went off on one. I couldn't get as much as a word in, and he was just going on about how he was the best in Europe, how he was the best in the world, and how he was going to beat me up and batter me. He was talking me down quite a lot, and that was new to me as well.'

It was the start of Hill being taken away from his normal routine, although the weigh-in stands out most. He had lost seven kilos that week, four and a half of those through dehydration, a lack of food, and an age in a sauna during the 24 hours before standing on the scales. As a result, he showed up exhausted, although that's not unusual when significant and strenuous efforts have been undertaken to make weight ahead of a fight. McGregor was unusual. He was hyper, getting into his face, shoving his head against Hill's, forcing him across the stage.

'I wasn't ready for it to kick off,' he says. 'The main thing that stood out for me … until that point, I just thought that Conor was a dickhead and all that talk was all just for show. One of the main things I see with fighters and sportsmen is a lot of the time, on social media, they'll talk crap and do it in person as well. They'll talk about what they're going to do and how now is their time and they are the very best. That's them lying to themselves. That's what I thought about Conor until the weigh-in, and it dawned on me.

'"Oh shit," I genuinely said to myself. "This guy believes everything. He's not all there."'

Hill had experiences of the fight-game bluster before. He asks not to name the opponent for obvious reasons, but on one previous occasion, he had another MMA exponent trash talking at him as well. This guy promised him what would happen, but then pulled out of the bout. Later, that fighter admitted to Hill that he wasn't in a good place mentally. It had basically all been an effort to get his friends and his camp to buy into his words about being the best, in the hope it would bounce back and he might believe it himself.

'That's what I thought Conor was doing,' Hill continues. 'Only then he squared up to me and starts shouting, "I'm going to fucking bury you. You look soft, you are soft." I just thought, "Shit, this isn't an act. This is what he really thinks." So initially, there's a little bit of intimidation. I knew he got a little lairy at weigh-ins, but it's a strange sensation. On one hand, even though you know the bloke is coming in there to try and knock your head off anyway, it's this that gets to you. Like, in dressing rooms, you know you are going out there, and if you overthink it, you'd realise, "This guy can legally punch or knee or kick or choke me, he is trying to break my limbs and take away my oxygen." But around that part of it, the adrenaline usually kicks in and it's quite surreal. A lot of times, what happens [is that] someone will say, "Remember when you landed that shot?" or "Do you remember when he took you down?" And you don't remember, as it's autopilot. As I got more experienced and fought more, I could keep my head together a bit more and was a bit more relaxed.

'After a while, I was more worried about losing, because you feel embarrassed rather than hurt. That's what I was scared and nervous about. All that work for eight weeks, and then you go home with nothing but your pride hurt. Because of that, with Conor, people wonder why his words mattered. It's hard to explain. But if I could go back and relive it, I would set myself up for it, as it gets in your head and makes you think too much. If someone comes to a weigh-in, shakes your hand, says, "See you tomorrow," you just go on and have a relaxing day. You're used to it. It's what you do. Sportsmanlike. But this? You think he means business, and after he said it, I wondered, "Do I look soft?" I remember people saying if I was alright, and I said I was fine. I think I'd have been better to confess and say that threw me a little bit, and gather my thoughts a little bit better.'

It put Hill on the back foot, and he stayed there.

Of their fight – after the talk – he recalls how McGregor could walk as well. Up to that point, what got Hill across the line so often was his fitness, meaning he stayed on the front foot and ground his opponent down with sheer work rate. But McGregor never took a backward step. He was on him from the start, stunting rhythm. If Hill tried to advance, he was caught with a shot, and suddenly it was McGregor doing what he wanted. And there was still talk there, too.

'He was quite a powerful presence. He's troubling me, and then he chatted a bit during the fight and that threw me as well. When we were up against the cage, he was saying, "You look soft, you look soft" and "I'll go all day with you." Part of me was concentrating on what I wanted to do in the fight, but another part was wondering, "Do I talk back?" When I fought, I never had someone speak to me like that. There's enough to be doing with trying to focus on the bout and listening to the cornerman, but now there's this.'

Ultimately, Hill submitted in round two for the only time ever. It was also a landmark for the victor as he hadn't just punched his opponent into submission, rather he showed a skill set and an evolution that many had thought he'd never make. McGregor even shook Hill's hand afterwards, sent him a few messages telling him to come over and train in Ireland, and the experience left Hill keeping a close eye. What took him aback most wasn't how far McGregor made it but rather that the same tactics in the lead-up to bouts had succeeded so far up the ladder.

'I'm surprised how much it's worked with others,' he says. 'Every time he's stepped up, especially when he started getting bigger name fighters, [Dustin] Poirier, a few of those guys. I thought there's no way he'll get inside their heads, as they are too experienced, they are too game. Then he did get in their head and did wind them up and did intimidate them. You could see it. They won't admit it, but I felt it worked. He did it even on José Aldo, threw him a little bit. I do think mentally he threw him, because people aren't used to it. In MMA, most people are very respectful which is a nice part of it. And then there's him. Whether intimidating or winding you up or getting you angry, it's an extra element.

'I don't think it worked with Khabib and Diaz, though. But most others, he got in their heads far more than expected. And it's nice to see him do so well, because he's the only person that ever stopped me when I was fighting, so at least I didn't lose to a mug. And I did start to find all his chatting entertaining, as much as I think sometimes it goes too far and he can be quite disrespectful. It does get too personal, but he backs it up and it's part of why he did so well. There is the odd case when I think, "What a dickhead," especially when he goes and loses. I don't think there's any shame in losing, but when you chat so much shit and call people out and then lose, it's humiliating. It doesn't help him when he's fighting top dogs.'

So what do you do with that crazy that Hill found so intimidating?

Take it away, and what is left come fight night?

Back then, in 2012, it was the perfect balance of madness and brilliance. The problem for McGregor is that the madness soon consumed him.

UFC was coming and, since then, when the final bell rings out, he no longer stops.

* * *

JOHN KAVANAGH WILL ALWAYS REMEMBER IT.

One day, a butterfly flapped its wings.

'Gunnar Nelson, my Icelandic fighter, was starting to make waves and I was considering moving there,' he recalled. 'But I got the call [a contract offer from UFC] and tried to phone Conor straight away. He wouldn't answer. He was teaching a boxing class for me at the time and hadn't shown for one of the sessions, and thought I was calling to eat him out of it. Eventually, he answers. "Sorry, John, I got delayed; the traffic was brutal." I said, "Shut up, will ye? It's not about that. UFC Sweden, eight weeks' time — we're on.'"

To this day he doesn't know how lucky they really were, or why that UFC call up really came about. For it was at that same time that Dana White had actually agreed to come to Trinity College in the heart of the city. Once about as far from a UFC crowd as possible, given the haughty origins and stuffy reputation of the place, it showed White once more how he'd made the sport more mainstream. But while there and during his stay in Dublin, those who were truly passionate about it also made White aware of how desperate they were to see McGregor make the step-up. He heard the message loud and clear and decided to give it a go.

He had a person in his company call Kavanagh.

Eight weeks on, and on a Tuesday morning in April 2013, McGregor stopped to collect his social welfare before going to the airport. There he met his coach and it all took off.

'Now it's a ten-car cavalcade wherever we go, but back then there was just the two of us. We get to Stockholm and we're walking through the hall, and there are all these teams and stars that I've been following for years, and I'm overwhelmed, thinking, "This is the UFC." But from the moment we got there, he walked taller than everybody. It was fascinating to watch. "Who's he? Put me in against him." He was aggressive, competitive, and ready to go at everybody. He grabbed it by the neck and he hasn't let go.'

It was there that famed cutman Stitch Duran would tell them the Irish were 'like the Mexicans on that side of the water, because you can fight, man'.

It was there, in a lift, that McGregor met Cub Swanson, one of the most exciting artists in the division at the time, and started to call him 'Cubby Bear.' He stared Swanson down for a while and told him he didn't keep himself in much shape between fights.

It was there that Marcus Brimage told him he needed to learn respect. It was there that he floored him and took back €60,000. It was there that it really began. Not just the athlete but all of it, including the creation of the modern McGregor. On the way back from Stockholm, and across the weeks that followed as he basked in glory, he swore it would never change him.

He had lied — this time not to Kavanagh over money, but to himself about life.

Having introduced Irish MMA to the world, those still here in his backyard speak of him as an embarrassment rather than the ambassador for it he once was.

Tommy Egan no longer speaks to him.

Coach Kavanagh these days keeps him at arm's length, preferring just to be around in his corner of the octagon for what he's good at, not for the mayhem he creates when he's out of it. On occasion, he's still rolled out to defend him: two years after their first interview, Paul Kimmage returned to talk to him, right after McGregor's recent loss to Nurmagomedov.

This time, it wasn't about playing up a prodigy but playing down the acts of an arsehole. Kimmage tells me, 'I like John. He has a kind heart and has done some great work with kids. I'm sure he has two views on McGregor — those he expressed to me and those he expresses privately.'

In public, however, Kavanagh defended McGregor jumping into the ring at Bellator in November 2017. 'He is very close to Charlie [Ward], and when he knocked the guy [John Redmond] out, he assumed, like we all did, that the fight was over. But the referee, Marc Goddard — the best in the world bar none — hadn't called it, and when Conor jumped over the cage, all hell broke loose. Again, it was absolutely the wrong thing to do. He acted like a jackass.'

He defended McGregor's attitude before an Irish court during a speeding hearing. 'Well, I wasn't at the court, I was in the gym, but if he did something wrong, why wasn't he prosecuted? He parked wrong? Someone should clamp him, take his car away. He's just a civilian. Am I going to sit down with him and say, "You should park your car the right way?" No, it's not me.'

He defended the 2018 attack on a bus in New York. 'He thought, "Do you know what? I'm going to go over there and be with Lobov." But he certainly didn't go over there with a plan. I know Conor. He doesn't plan. He went over with good intentions but ended up in a position where he spent a night in jail and brought the sport into disrepute. And he has been punished, legally and financially, for that.'

He defended his legacy. 'I'm saying that it's a parent's job to point out the good parts and the bad. Conor has incredible role model qualities — dedication, self-belief, hard work, intelligence. He's created this industry. No one was making money out of MMA, not real money, not Federer money. Federer could be quiet as a mouse, have zero personality, and never give an interview in his life, and he'd still be guaranteed tens of millions every year through sponsorships. That's not possible in MMA. You're fighting for fifty grand.'

It's said a society grows great when old men plant trees whose shade they know they shall never sit in. Maybe there's still time for him to sow, but it's quickly running out.

CHAPTER 7

GOD

A PLANNED VEGAS EVENING IN, AND *NETWORK* CROPS up on the television in the hotel room. Anywhere in the world, it's among the better reasons you'll find to keep it an evening in.

For those who've come across the 1970s Oscar-winning movie, there's a remarkable scene where TV station chairman Arthur Jensen is confronting news anchor Howard Beale. He rants and he raves, pronouncing a misunderstanding by the common person about how the world works.

'You are an old man who thinks in terms of nations and peoples,' he stresses. 'There are no nations. There are no peoples. There are no Russians. There are no Arabs. There are no third worlds. There is no west. There is only one holistic system of systems, one vast and immane, interwoven, interacting, multivariate, multinational dominion of dollars. Petro-dollars, electro-dollars, multi-dollars, reichmarks, rins, rubles, pounds, and shekels. It is the international system of currency which determines the totality of life on this planet. That is the natural order of things today. That is the atomic and sub-atomic and galactic structure of things today. And you have meddled with the primal forces of nature, and you will atone. Am I getting through to you…'

A terrified Beale is informed by Jensen that he is the man to deliver this message to the people, given his status as a famous TV presenter. Ultimately staring up, Beale proclaims, 'I have seen the face of God.'

'You just might be right,' concludes Jensen.

It's a powerful few moments, oozing an ultra-capitalism similar to this city McGregor and I find ourselves in the midst of, a place where everyone lands in with what little they've cobbled together, are duped by the professional sell, exploited by the professional hustle, and that money makes its way up under the guise of a wealth transfer masquerading as a little bit of harmless fun.

In essence there's enough for everybody here, but that's still not enough for some.

There was a story from a cabbie the other night that surmises so much about the city. He said, 'Nobody is really from Vegas, rather they all just get trapped here.' He himself is from California, came for a weekend of play and games a full fifteen years ago, and lost so much that he's been driving around ever since paying it back, bit by bit.

The reminders are all over. Going to a chemist for a new toothbrush, a woman on one of those scooters for the obese overtakes me going in the door. She's not here for medication to rid herself of an illness, but to indulge that illness. It's 8.15am, and the casinos are five minutes away at her top speed, yet those seconds aren't for wasting. It's here she comes out of convenience to sit at the slot machines. Across the road, having bought a three-litre bottle of water to rehydrate, another woman comes jogging from her car with a smaller and empty bottle. She starts into a frantic explanation about how they used to refill it for her for nothing, but they now want 50 cent, and if she might siphon some off. Inside a corner shop the tough looking red-head woman behind the counter grabs everyone's attention when letting out a roar. 'Is your mouth on my relish,' she screams. The kid putting sauce on his sandwich is caught trying to bite off the top but rather than the slightest flicker of shame or contrition, he removes the communal bottle from his gob and screams back. 'I'm opening it with my mouth. I've got no Goddamn nails.'

Against such a backdrop, there's a notion that still prevails today that sport is somehow an escape from all of this. An afternoon off. A weekend away. A break from it.

This is hugely misguided for sport is a part of it. And UFC is yet one more arrow in the quiver.

It's little wonder this place is where brothers Lorenzo and Frank Fertitta landed and thrived. It was in 2001 when the duo took over UFC and applied the same logic as they did to their casinos. It wasn't about blood on the canvas, as those in the octagon were mere employees. What mattered was how productive — or unproductive — those employees were to the bottom line.

For MMA, the journey to that point is so complex that it can be hard to know exactly where to start. It was in Japan that, over hundreds of years, jiu-jitsu was developed among the exclusivity of the samurai. Their aim was to have a skill that, when stripped of their weapons, would allow them to take down and kill armed enemies. Hidden away, it wasn't until the nineteenth century that this art became more mainstream, allowing access to people from different classes and backgrounds. But there was still one inhibiting factor: size. One would-be fighter, Kanō Jigorō, was simply too small at 5ft 2in and 90 pounds. However, like many with a syndrome around just that, he wouldn't be told no.

Jigorō started to study other forms of combat, from western wrestling to sumo, taking in different grappling techniques that would give him an advantage around taking down larger opponents. He would use their size and shape against them so effectively that at one point, he was invited to give a demonstration before US president Ulysses S. Grant. It was a major evolution, as it wasn't just about diving straight in but about different pulls and pushes to take others by surprise and knock them off balance. Then, on the ground, he would could use choking techniques.

This was the foundation of what would become judo.

Over time, Jigorō passed on his knowledge to pupil Mitsuyo Maeda, and he in turn took it with him on a journey across the west. First to the United States, on to Cuba, through Central and South America, before finally shacking up in Brazil. Travel and chance: it would bring MMA a step closer.

It was there, in Rio de Janeiro in the 1910s, that businessman and diplomat Gastão Gracie was having trouble with his son. Carlos Gracie may have been a rich kid, but he acted like a street thug and was always happy to brawl. So, Gastão hired Maeda to instil some discipline. From this meeting, Brazilian jiu-jitsu was born. A long line of the Gracie family would go on to engage in what's known as *vale tudo*, translating as 'anything goes', with fights allowing for pretty much the lot, bar biting and eye gouging.

Initially, any public bouts played out in circuses, and customers saw it as one more oddity under the big top, with the *Japanese-American Courier* informing on 4 October 1928: 'One report from Brazil declares that jiu-jitsu is truly an art and that in an interesting exhibition in the side tent to the big circus a Bahian of monstrous dimensions met his Waterloo at the hands of a diminutive Japanese wrestler. The man was an expert at Capoeira, an old South American style of fighting, but after putting the Japanese on his back and trying to kick his head ... the little oriental by the use of a jiu-jitsu hold threw the Bahian and after a short struggle he was found sitting on the silent frame of the massive opponent.'

Little seeds.

It took until the early 1960s for it to dare enter the mainstream, with the latest generations of the Gracie family behind match-making and getting fights onto Rio de Janeiro television. Even then there were problems, though, and their slot was removed by executives when an arm bar was used one night. The man caught in it refused to submit, meaning his arm was eventually snapped on camera to a horrified audience at home. Jiu-jitsu was driven out from under the lights into the underground, where a subculture formed.

The Gracies, however, were always relentless and refused to give up. With so many styles incorporated and contrasted in the ring, with time served away from that mainstream, and with money to be made, they returned in the era of pay-per-view. It's why in November of 1993, the Ultimate Fighting Championship took place, thanks to Rorion Gracie's marketing skills and Art Davie's influence. The prize fund was $50,000, with eight competitors set to do battle. These included Gerard Gordeau, a Dutch karate champion who didn't always play by the rules; Teila Tuli, a giant sumo wrestler from Hawaii; and Art Jimmerson, a good but not great boxer from LA with a 29-5 sweet science record.

There was Royce Gracie too, who came across Ken Shamrock in the semi-final. Despite giving up forty pounds, he used the techniques that Jigorō had put together more than a century before and which Maeda had brought to his family. He went on to fight Gordeau in the final and, after having his ear bitten by the Dutch man, took revenge by holding onto the choke well after his opponent had tapped out. In fact, there were sixteen taps in total.

It was a freak show that drew looks out of curiosity rather than awe. But not everyone who had watched it was pleased. Senator John McCain famously called it 'human cock-fighting' and started a campaign to have it banned. He was a big boxing fan, and his wife was a big player in Anheuser-Busch, who had pumped millions upon millions into the boxing industry, but the conflict of interest didn't stop him.

When Shamrock and Dan Severn fought at UFC 9, new rules were enforced by the courts, meaning they couldn't strike with closed fists and if they tried to they'd be arrested by the local authorities. They need not have worried as, with Severn circling Shamrock in the middle of the ring and no shots thrown, at one point referee John McCarthy was forced to step in and suspend the match. As the commentary put it, 'These are two of the greatest fighters in the world, but they're not fighting.'

McCain continued his campaign thereafter, getting pay-per-view cards pulled from networks as arenas refused to rent out their space. UFC was in trouble.

That is until 2001, when the Fertitta brothers came on board.

Their family had originally come from Galveston, Texas, where they'd married into the Maceo family, who were running gambling and prostitution rings in the city. Under pressure from the law, they moved to Vegas and started a successful casino empire. The brothers were the inheritors of this fortune, and it allowed them to give MMA a go. Their deal was helped along by their friend Dana White, a boxercise instructor who said he had to flee Boston after the late and infamous gangster Whitey Bulger tried to extort from him. There has been much scepticism around these claims.

Of course they had other help, too. The Fertittas were well in with the Republican party who quickly aided in easing sanctions on the sport, and the Unified Rules brought in a structure which also improved appearance. All they then needed was an arena to host their fights. The Trump Taj Mahal in Atlantic City was the place in which they found a home.

As White said on stage at a presidential rally before the 2016 election, 'Nobody took us seriously except Donald Trump. He was the first guy to recognise the potential in the UFC that we saw, and encouraged us to build our business. Donald championed the UFC before it was popular, before it grew into a successful business, and I'll always be so grateful to him for standing with us in those early days. So tonight, I stand with Donald Trump. So let's be honest, we need someone who believes in this country, is proud of this country, and will fight for this country.'

It was a unique insight into how the long-time outsiders who had found themselves hidden out of view were suddenly siding with the right wing, as the disenfranchised more and more backed those that disenfranchised them.

It didn't happen overnight, mind. In fact, it didn't initially happen in the octagon. The early years were a slog, so much so that the Fertittas thought about cutting their losses for a while. Instead, though, they tapped into the booming reality television market and by 2005, they launched The Ultimate Fighter. If it's a good enough springboard to elect the leader of the free world ... In this instance, the winners, it was advertised, would get a six-figure contract. But this being a new era of the UFC, the small print actually said that the contract was split over three years and the full amount wouldn't be paid unless the winner won every bout in that time. What you don't know can't hurt you, though, and those tuning in didn't care about such details. It worked. Much went in the UFC's favour outside of its power, too.

Pride in Japan had been the main MMA organisation but, in 2003, the president of their ownership company, Naoto Morishita, was found hanged in his hotel room, allegedly after his mistress had said she wanted to end their affair. There was speculation also that it may have been due to tax issues and links to the Yakuza. All the while, some tabloids led speculation that Pride was in fact a front for the Yakuza. It ruined the image of the company and it ruined its relationships. Fuji TV finally walked away due to contract breaches, and that was the defining blow. The UFC itself stepped in and bought Pride, but such was the reputational damage that had long been done, they couldn't keep it afloat either.

In 2007, Pride closed, meaning there was only one MMA superpower left.

A year on and the economic crash came. A sport that was once about counter-culture suddenly and instead became a hitching post for angry men. They were far more mainstream than the Fight Club-esque base of before, helped out by mythical rope-a-dope-esque storylines like Anderson Silva's victory over Chael Sonnen. A perfect storm.

As a result it grew, while the United States economy shrunk.

And it grew through exploitative business methods, too.

* * *

THE NOISES AND MESSAGE OF *NETWORK*, OF LAS VEGAS, of the UFC, and of McGregor bounced around across a sleepless night. There's some salvation though.

Come morning, and Jacob 'Stitch' Duran is waiting over breakfast.

He knows this side of this game better than most. A long-time cutman around these parts, he's on time to the second. After years of working on farms in California, he says he realised that decency and respect meant more than anything you had in your wallet. 'If you ate it, I probably picked it,' he recalls of his first job. 'Cotton, apricots, grapes, figs, peppers, peaches.'

It was there he also learned about workers' rights, and that would later see him booted from the UFC. 'Growing up as a farm-hand, we had no protection and we were fighting for rights. We have a theory: we have so many pesticides in us that mosquitoes don't bite us no more. And my parents were strong into the Cesar Chavez movement and doing the right thing for the farm workers, so when the rights came up with the UFC, I thought about it and said my parents would be disappointed if I didn't stand up and do the right thing.'

Long before the right thing, for Duran there were a lot of other things on the road less travelled. He wanted to be a pro baseball player but ended up in the air force instead. Based in Thailand, he went to a kickboxing match one night so long ago he can't even tell you the year, saw a guy knocked out by a boot to the neck, and wanted in. Nearby, some Koreans taught taekwondo. When they moved on, the locals replaced it with Muai Thai. Finally returning home, Andre Ward, who he'd known since a kid, said he wanted him to be his cutman if he ever went pro.

Thus first came boxing. He was even Wladimir Klitschko's cutman when he fought Lennox Lewis in *Ocean's Eleven* and, as a result, ended up in his corner for the real bout with DaVarryl Williamson in 2004. The Ukrainian needed his help before he even walked out: throwing punches in his dressing room, he had caught himself in the nose and busted it open.

As for UFC, Duran had known Dana White from around the Vegas gyms and got talking to him one night. 'I was always training A-level fighters; he wasn't at that A level, not even at the B level. He says he was in boxing but to a small extent. But I was doing a K-1 at the Bellagio. I see him in the audience and he says to hit him up, and I did the next day. Lo and behold, he told me they bought the UFC and asked if I'd be a cutman. I knew nothing about MMA, really, if I'm honest. But we were just talking the other day. At the beginning, everybody had a name. Dana said, "Stitch, we are gonna do this and that, and when we make money, you'll all make money."

'Well, they made money, but we didn't make money. I worked corporate America and understand the business philosophy of a corporate company, and I appreciate it. But there were some things in the mix that didn't make sense to me. Sponsorship was the final straw. They took away fighters' sponsorship but gave them x-amount based on how many fights they had in the UFC in this Reebok deal,' he notes of the footwear and apparel company coming on board in a sort of catch-all sponsorship effort. Indeed what that did was remove the individual deals and income that those involved had arranged themselves, as Reebok's name and logo would now be everywhere and on everyone, with the proceeds going to the UFC and some of it dripping on down from there. 'In the UFC and during that era, fighters were making a lot of money out of their sponsorship. A lot more than what the UFC were paying. With the cutmen, they said, "You guys get rid of your sponsors too and we can't compensate." I was looking at this and thinking, "The ring girls get more than us, but who is more important?" I tried to meet them, and the story was there's no money in the kitty and that's the end of it. At that point, the fans were bitching and moaning.'

It was part of a UFC effort to draw the curtain across the brutality and instead present itself as a somewhat sanitised and corporate product, just as the NFL had done. A clean-cut and professional front was the bean-counters' way into expansion and more profit. But when Duran got a call from a journalist, he decided he'd be honest and speak openly about this move. 'Next, a friend of mine called, he says because of the interview I did, the UFC was not going to use me anymore. I wasn't going to bust his balls, he's a friend. So I said, "Alright, do me a favour. You tell Dana he ain't got no balls to call me in person."

'Dust started settling and a couple of weeks later, UFC does a big show on Fox. Dana is being interviewed and was asked if I'd ever be back, and he said no. He added that him and I were never friends. That slapped him in the face,' stresses Duran, regarding the reaction White got for hanging out such a popular character to dry. 'Just the entire way he handled that situation. It didn't bother me. That's over four years now, and people still stop me. It got so bad that the guy from Reebok called and tried to be apologetic and said they'd nothing to do with it.'

He still had a chance to come across McGregor, though, during his 2013 debut in Stockholm. Duran saw this white guy getting ready in the locker room. So he called out that the Irish were the Mexicans, only on the other side of the Atlantic. 'You guys can fight and they can fight.'

'John Kavanagh always kept that in mind,' he says. 'I worked his bout when he was in Boston after. Very humble, very polite but the kid could fight. Tremendous, but I think the value he brought to the UFC, he transitioned it. I think Conor is a master of what he does and of marketing. I left the store a minute ago before I came here, and a lady was asking if I was going to go to McGregor-Khabib, and McGregor's name is always first.

'But in that transition, he's changed what is done in the UFC. He said, "I've my own promotion company," and negotiated the proper things for him to maximise his dollars. I think that's given other fighters the opportunity. They say, "Conor opened this door, I'll go through; you've got to pay me what I'm worth." But he probably saved the UFC from going down, too. So I gotta say props to Conor. I know a lot of people don't like him, but the bottom line – like Mayweather – you can talk all the shit you want so long as you can back it up. He's seriously impressive. I like his style, it's unorthodox but it's gutsy. He's on the outside using his hands, and he has all the fighting qualities to be at where he's at.'

Of course, Duran's experiences mean he's not only looking back but looking in with unbiased perspective. Granted, to limit his thoughts on MMA and on McGregor to just the numbers is to miss a trick. After all, Frank Mir has said of him that when he sees the cutman walk into a dressing room his heart sinks, as he knows it's time to fight. Vitor Belfort has said that his presence brings a calming effect. That realm, getting ready to walk into a place where your opponent's aim is to basically render you unconscious through a knockout or a choke that starves the brain of oxygen, is unnerving simply to imagine.

But right now, McGregor's getting ready to do it again against Nurmagomedov.

He's made the sell, which is the easy part.

What he's signed up to is truly terrifying.

Duran takes me into the headspace in those moments. 'I keep in mind, once I sit the fighter down and start wrapping hands, that is their first step in going into battle. On a psychological level, I try and cheer them up, and make them laugh. Even the Russians, which is the hardest. I give them a hug and let them know I'm there to cover their back. It's a very special moment. I've had guys cry when wrapping their hands, I've had guys joke around like it's nothing. I get to see those moments and to me, they're priceless.'

I ask about this McGregor fight next week, and of course it is something he's seen before. 'We always say, "In boxing, the only thing that counts is the truth." You can beat anything, but you can't beat time — and the thing about McGregor is, going from rags to riches at warp speed, it changes lifestyle and personality. All that time he was off, did it take a lot of his fighting spirit from him? It's a lot easier not to train hard when you know you don't have to. Conor might verbally and physically still give the impression he has it, but when it comes to the late rounds, does that take effect? I personally think it will.

'Just because you're at the top doesn't mean the guys below you aren't the best. They just haven't gotten to that level or had that chance to show it,' he explains. 'Around this, look at entourages. I hate them and I see it with Conor. You feel important, but they are useless. You, your trainer, your cutman, your manager, that's all you ever need. It's a simple game. You go into anything further than that and it's stupid money spent. They are only kissing the guy's ass. So many have made so much money, they always thought there'd be tomorrow, and it never came and they buy all this stuff. Clingers on.

'Mike Tyson, we used to all train in the same gym. When Mike was at the top, it looked like a caravan of cars arriving. Ridiculous stuff. One guy would carry his bag, another would take his clothes out, another would put his shoes on. Bullshit like that. All of that cost Mike a hell of a lot of money. They all had phones, expenses. In summer, they'd leave his car running the whole time he was training. You could have done it ten minutes before the end and it'd be cold. But as he was coming down, no more entourage.'

How many times have we heard that story?

The reason is usually the same despite the fact that outside company and material possessions have never filled the void. A few years back when Tim Keown of ESPN went to meet Floyd Mayweather, he found him in a jewellery store, surrounded by his entourage opening duffle bags filled with $100 bills as he wore $3m in platinum and diamonds, while two Gulfstream private jets sat in waiting on Teterboro's tarmac across the road. In McGregor, Mayweather had a kindred spirit: before the bout between the pair, when the *Guardian's* Donald McRae went to meet the Dubliner, he was left waiting in the airport before his subject showed up in a rented sports car and proceeded to drive him up and down the Las Vegas strip for the duration of their interview in a false show of opulence. While the figures and worlds they inhabit may differ, there is a key similarity. It revolves around a massive insecurity of ego that means they demand constant attention, as the silence scares them.

Duran tells another story about Tyson that's relevant to every fighter who follows the same career curve. Doing a documentary many years ago that was met with little interest when he tried to pitch it, he interviewed the most dangerous man on the planet and threw out a fascinating question. 'What's the one little ingredient every top fighter has?'

The response was just as fascinating. 'They take the pain,' Tyson said. He wasn't just referring to the literal pain that comes with the physical aspect of the job, as significant as that is. He was referring to everything that comes with being a top fighter: the stress and strain on relations with family and friends; the sudden requirement to deal with wealth previously unimaginable; the pressures of being catapulted into the limelight in an instant.

Does Conor McGregor still want the pain?

Can Conor McGregor still take that pain?

Has Dana White ever wondered about that aspect of him, too?

Outside the Barclays Centre back in February 2018, after McGregor and his entourage attacked that bus with Khabib and others, it was fitting that White should rush to the scene and hype it up with attention-grabbing outrage. 'The most disgusting thing that has ever happened in the history of the company.'

Just as McGregor alluded to at the start of his career on Irish television, shock gets attention and attention makes money. This was a time when investigations by the likes of Bloomberg showed UFC to be in difficulty, with experts saying the model wasn't sustainable. White added that he would never do business with McGregor again, but never believe a salesman, which is exactly what he is.

Now, with the countdown on to fight night, the promo is worth a look.

Front and centre is that very same incident with McGregor allegedly losing his mind in an underground car park, smashing glass with metal.

UFC replaces pain with gain. From cries of 'disgusting' to one more expensive McGregor grudge match.

'I have seen the face of God.'

You just might be right, Mr White.

CHAPTER 8

CHASING SHADOWS

IN DUBLIN, THERE'S SOMETHING A LITTLE OFF ON this January morning.

It's not so much that most people who know him don't like to speak on the record about Conor McGregor. Instead, it's that so many agree to chatter, disappear for a while, then a little while more, and either come back with a change of heart or keep on ignoring calls. Enough follow the same routine to the point where it's hard not to think it's staged.

At worst, it's done to waste time, at best it's because he and therefore those around him are so controlling of content and image. It's difficult not to lean towards the latter when considering his own past actions. Take, for instance, that Mayweather sham when his team contacted

ESPN and suggested they could produce his content around the bout for €100,000. Can you imagine Kobe Bryant doing that? Then there was the bus incident in New York, when he had one of his team call a journalist merely doing their job by reporting on the story. 'Conor wants you to know he sees everything,' they said in threatening tones.

The arrogance of it all. Does he not realise that the world sees everything *he* does, and that not getting arrested might be a better approach than trying to intimidate those reporting his arrest? You would have to be pretty far gone and pretty far removed from reality not to get that. It's as if he can no longer control himself, so he tries to control everything else. The fact that so many cancel meetings and interviews is a testament to this.

John Kavanagh, at least, is decent about it. Around the time of McGregor's first UFC win, he was more than accommodating when it came to getting his fighter some publicity – the sort that was plenty scarce in both Ireland and the wider mainstream sports media. It was soon after in 2013 that I asked again to talk with Conor, this time for a feature about sportspeople and their tattoos. Yet on that occasion, the reply had centred around how McGregor was in demand and far too big to be dealing with such petty requests from his homeland. The transformation had begun, and it soon enveloped those around him.

Move on a few months, and with McGregor abusing and insulting many, I began calling him out on it, talking about how he was clearly moving away from being a decent character and how this likely wouldn't end well. It was then that Kavanagh decided the previous email request was a sign of grovelling and posted it online with my mobile at the bottom. Abuse from supporters began in an instant, swelling until a new phone number was required.

'I sometimes think of our exchanges back when I was just beginning to deal with the media and regret how emotional I became,' Kavanagh now tells me. 'I was just learning how that world worked. I am a lot more familiar with it now. I'll be straight with you and say I've zero interest in doing an interview based on Conor. I gave a recent exhaustive one [to Paul Kimmage]. As expected, a bunch of quotes were pulled out of it for a number of sub-articles, some slightly altered for the myriad of MMA websites out there, and used to generate clickbait. The next time I do an interview mentioning him will be in the build-up to his next contest, should he decide to fight again. Have a good day.'

Andrew McGahon was one of the first journalists around McGregor. They became friends, he worked for his Mac Life site and warns, 'I'd have to check out if people involved were cool with me talking about it while currently being so close to the situation. And I'd hate for someone to feel I was talking on behalf of Conor or out of line.' He does check it out and agrees, but then does a U-turn: 'I have ditched social media. I am in the process of removing myself from this line of work and putting all my time and energy into my own competing, so I'm gonna have to rule myself out.'

His photographer Dave Fogarty and members of McGregor's training circle go to ground. Former teammate Aisling Daly gets in touch, the woman he floored when he first entered the Straight Blast gym. She agrees to converse, passes on her number, then ignores all contact over many weeks. Even PR manager Lynn Hunter and her agency that dealt with Conor in Ireland, and still deal with his father, cannot be bothered to respond to requests.

Their silences and attitudes are arguably more insightful than any interview. What gets out is supposed to be solely what Conor wants to get out, always feeding the myth, always adding to the marketed monster, always slipping and slithering away from a truth that, for some reason, he cannot tolerate.

Out of all of them though, there is one person I do genuinely want to speak to, but he is also elusive. Either that, or his operation is all over the place. His manager and agent, Audie Attar, was born in Iraq, moved to the States and got lucky aged only two and was lucky to get out alive when holidaying in his birthplace as George HW Bush first tried to teach a lesson to Saddam Hussein. In 2009, he founded Paradigm Sports Management Agency, and in 2013 got in touch with McGregor around his UFC debut. Many will say he hitched his wagon to that horse since. It's hard to know what to believe, though. Is he a marketing genius? Or is he just lucky?

For instance, the story goes that a few weeks before Attar put in that call, McGregor nearly signed with an Irish agent who was offering €1,000 a month while looking for around a quarter of his fight earnings in return. He avoided that disaster, but how much of what followed is Attar's creation and how much is it McGregor's natural progression?

So many questions. So much mystery.

'I got in touch with McGregor after the UFC breakthrough,' Attar previously explained. 'People were like, "You should look at him, he's really special." We looked at some clips from Cage Warriors, and I watched him and I was like, "This kid is something else." His hand-eye co-ordination, his depth perception, his ability to get in and out and land shots so cleanly, I thought he was very, very special. And for a 145er, I'm like, "This guy is fucking huge." Size, speed, age — everything you want about the kid was there. There wasn't charisma like he's portrayed now. I would tell you that the first time we're on the phone, he's funny. He's just funny, a charismatic personality, and then he beats Brimage and does the "60gs, baby" [a message he left for Dana White in the octagon following his first victory, referencing how much money he was now owed]. That was funny, and you start to see bits and pieces of it.'

After numerous calls to Attar's California office, however, and it starts to feel like one of those companies that's really no more than a PO Box on the Isle of Man. Finally, an assistant does respond via email. 'Mr Attar is travelling and unable to respond to your inquiry.

Should anything change I will be in touch.' I reply to say that there's no rush and that I am more than happy to try and talk with him when he's done travelling.

You want to like Attar in terms of the person and the agent, even if that agency is named after what he says was 'a personal paradigm shift from a hot-headed underachiever to focused professional'. Aside from such corporate nonsense, though, his story is good. He went to UCLA and played as a linebacker. He was good at it too, and during his time there the UCLA Bruins football team won a Pac-10 championship and made appearances in the Rose Bowl and Sun Bowl, two of the better end-of-season games based on performance in American college football. Then, shortly after 9/11, he was in a bar near campus, bumped into a customer, got an anti-Muslim comment spat back at him, and off came the gloves.

'Our society changed,' Attar said of that bust-up that saw him booted from his UCLA team. 'The way I was looked at changed. One thing led to another and it turned into an altercation. So here I am saying I'm defending myself, but as a high-level, testosterone-fuelled athlete, you have more strength. So, the fight didn't last too long. But then that causes issues and people tried to take advantage of that situation ... There wasn't much racial tension toward Arabs until this [9/11] happened. Now I'm afraid the number of people harmed because of this tragedy will escalate. America isn't about being white. It's the land of the free where everyone comes together to fulfil [their] dreams.'

It sounds like a healthy attitude, but as with most things near McGregor, there's an issue.

To see and to understand that, you just need one tale to show the trajectory and where he's ending up.

* * *

PAULIE MALIGNAGGI CAN TALK.

And talk.

And talk.

He might even talk better than he boxed, which is saying something. In fact, as he begins to work himself up in anger, he starts to come across like a Sopranos character flying into a rage in the mirror. For that reason, he says, he doesn't tell the story about his encounter with McGregor often, because in order to be fair and accurate he needs to get into every little detail.

I tell him to work away, that I have all day. So make of this what you will.

Some years back, he came across and made friends with Irish welterweight Dean Byrne in the Wild Card Gym in Los Angeles. He hadn't heard from him for a while but got a call in April 2017 asking if Dean's brother Gerry, a part of McGregor's team, might get in touch and if he might pass on his number. He said to go for it. It was no problem whatsoever.

Then came silence.

A former world welterweight champion that had retired to a TV analysis job in the United States, he didn't give it any more thought but, come June, Gerry Byrne did finally get in touch. With McGregor beginning his preparations for the Floyd Mayweather bout, he asked about the chance of Malignaggi coming to camp as a sparring partner.

Then came yet more silence.

In the end, Malignaggi was hired to do the North American leg of the press tour for Showtime and still there was nothing. When it finished, it was late July. Gerry Byrne did get back in touch and firmed up some dates that were only days away. Out of shape, Malignaggi thought about it and, having been in many camps, recalled how those brought in only tended to do three or four rounds anyway. Fascinated by being part of it all, and getting a rare insight into what was to be a pay-per-view record breaker, he agreed.

While McGregor was busy talking about his cardio, while his team talked about him bringing something new to a near-ancient sport, while the UFC and any around them were busy exploiting fans who ought to have seen truth, this was that actual reality.

'I got there on the Wednesday and we did eight rounds on Thursday,' Malignaggi remembers. 'It was uneventful. He wasn't that good; I was out of shape. I wasn't trying to win rounds but I could still control the pace. I guess the start of the experience was all pretty much fine except for the house. It was dingy. It had one TV, no channels; you had to use Wi-fi. It was in a ghetto in Vegas, but that wasn't where his main team was staying. He was in his own house with Kavanagh and the coaches and Gerry. The rest of the sparring team were in this shithole. I wasn't asking to be treated anyway special, though. I could have easily asked them to put me in the MGM Grand, but whatever. They'd offered, I took it, and I never complained. I just got on with it, I was there to spar and help Conor.

'He seemed normal at first. In the ring, he talked a lot of trash, but so be it. Although, for the sparring sessions he hired Joe Cortez, the retired referee. He wanted to get used to the boxing rules and the psychology of a full fight atmosphere. So he wanted centre ring, a touch of gloves, instructions. It was kind of corny the first time and I thought it was a joke. I was trying not to laugh at this, wondering "Is this guy for real?" But we did the rounds anyway and after sparring he said he was pleased with it, and he'd like me to stay and help out if possible. I said, "Okay, that's a plan. We'll work it out."

'That was it on Thursday. We were supposed to spar again on Saturday as I was leaving on Monday for Adrien Broner-Mikey Garcia. I figured they'd get two sessions out of me before I went away. Saturday came and he didn't want to spar me, he wanted to spar this journeyman Dashon Johnson and this amateur kid Tiernan Bradley. Which, well, whatever, I'm not training for a fight. I didn't think I'd gone hard two days prior, though. But the fact he didn't use me as much as he could before I left, that confirmed what I suspected about his character. I watched him lose to Nate Diaz and the choices he made — he lacked character. It was less work for me with a base salary so I didn't question him, but he is going to fight Floyd Mayweather. Why not try and get the best out of himself?'

The saying in boxing goes that you suffer in camp so you don't have to on fight night. Based on that, this story didn't add up.

What also didn't add up was a photo McGregor made public of himself with his hands behind his back during their rounds. It meant that everything Malignaggi was asked back on press duty came back to this and how good McGregor was. For the most part, he toed the line but on occasion, he let the truth, as he saw it, slip. 'I took it as, "Ah whatever. People get the gist." But the following weekend in New York, the media wanted details. They weren't even talking about the fight I was actually there to work on, a big fight. I had to dodge missiles. I had to not make myself look bad, but they were asking stupid questions. "Is he beating you up?" I had to defend my image and defend his. I'm getting bombarded, I'm working, I have no choice. It was constantly, "How hard does this guy hit?"

'I've been hit so many times, in my fights, gyms, sparring. I gave an honest answer. I said, "He's like a grown man and that has to be respected." That he doesn't hit hard or soft. Now he wanted me to say he hits like Golovkin. If it's closer to Golovkin or my sister, it's closer to my sister. When Miguel Cotto hit me, I was wondering if it was real. I'd sparred Amir Imam, a prospect, a good puncher. We had sixteen-ounce gloves, and still he hits light years above what McGregor did or could. I'd have to check if I was still standing at times when I was in with him. But I didn't say anything offensive. I tried to dodge it, but sometimes an answer came out. I said you had to respect it. That was the total context.'

Back he went to Vegas, to what he describes as 'the crack house'. He was unpacking in his room that night when one of the other sparring partners came in and told him he was going to be set up the next day. What did it mean? Well, in McGregor's camps, nothing is ever scheduled. You are booked for the day, and you may or may not be used. Either way, you won't know until it's upon you, but it had been decided in the background. The next day, he would be told ringside to go the full twelve rounds. To Malignaggi, it seemed a waste of time. Why would McGregor prepare for a fight by sparring one out of shape boxer for twelve rounds when he could have a number of them alternating? That way he would always be facing a fresh opponent.

But nonetheless he showed up to the UFC training centre, and where the upstairs room was usually deserted, there was a relatively large crowd of about twenty. They were high profile too, although more had been expected, with the likes of Gordon Ramsey not taking up an invite.

'At that point, I realised it was malice,' Malignaggi says. 'I got there, and the crowd is bigger but the rest is the usual. Everything is so controlled. You have to put your phone in a bag in case anyone tries to sneak footage. [McGregor] was about twenty minutes late as normal. I was warming up hard. I wanted to kick his ass. He arrives. He's cool. Friendly. He gets to the gym, shakes my hand. But he's such a two-faced guy. We start, and I tried to get off to a fast start and he held his own. After four or five rounds, I was thinking, "I'm not going to make this full twelve."

'Then something funny happened. He started to tire in front of me. The middle rounds, he started getting his ass kicked. On the basis of that confidence, I bit down and stayed. He doesn't like getting hit, and he was in better shape but can't handle getting beat up. I was yelling at him, at his corner, at Dana White. I was telling them what a fraud he was and a lot more. I'd tell you what I was saying, but I'd probably lose my media job if I repeated it. He landed a few good shots but the only reason that day he didn't get stopped was because I couldn't follow up my attacks. I'd land but wasn't in the shape to go in for a bit more. But I was getting time between the exchanges and I could recover. He'd be stopped if I was in better shape — as no matter who, he folds when getting hit.'

They made it to the end, to applause from the room. If there was any tension before, Malignaggi was sure they'd beaten it out of each other and beaten respect into one another. He was pleased with himself, too: one thing in fighting is that if you have to be in good shape to give a whooping over twelve rounds, you have to be in better shape to take one. He knew he wasn't at his best physically, therefore he couldn't have taken a beating.

At worst, he claims, he held his own, to the point where White came up and said he appreciated him being there and helping out, though Malignaggi brushed past him, wanting to give no time to a man who, in his opinion, treated his own fighters so poorly. Instead he headed for the dressing rooms, telling McGregor he needed to stop with the public pictures.

'I'm only saying this: I know you are trying to promote the fight, but I have to constantly field questions if you put out these pictures,' he said. 'Last week was tough.'

'You liked it,' retorted McGregor.

If Malignaggi had expected a normal answer, this wasn't it.

Instead, McGregor, in a towel and without turning, headed for the showers and roared, 'I don't know, Paulie, we got some good footage of the last couple of rounds.'

'I'm waiting for him to say he's kidding, but he turns the corner and that's it,' adds Malignaggi. 'I was like, "Is this guy serious?" I just said, "Alright Conor, you do that [and] I'll be telling the truth about all of this, if that's the path you want to go down." He didn't answer. I didn't shower, I was so angry. I dried off, went downstairs, back to the house.'

The next morning, he checked his phone and got a direct message from McGregor, a shot of him on the canvas after what he says was a slip. Thinking no more about it, he went about his day in Vegas, visiting Frank Mir and meandering around the city.

'What more am I supposed to think?' he says of the image. 'It was a slip. Cortez was referee and is motioning no knockdown. Also, knockdowns in gyms are super rare considering the thousands of rounds. Gloves are too big, there's headgear, guys are alternating in and out. In my lifetime, I've been knocked down four or five times in twenty years. Slips, falls, that happens all the time. But when there's a legit knockdown, there's a huge reaction. So that was it.'

Until the next day.

Another sparring session, he was again on standby. A text came through telling those in his house to be at the training centre for three. So Malignaggi goes, warms up hard, as he's sore from the twelve rounds and wants to work off the pain. McGregor again shows 25 minutes after he said he would, with his trainers, and they say he's not sparring anyone.

'This is a guy fighting Floyd Mayweather,' thought Malignaggi, not for the first time.

With his hands wrapped, he decided he'd do some bag work himself and asked the striking coach Owen Roddy to glove him up. Instead, he and the others were told they were to go downstairs, where there was no real equipment available to them. Roddy said they had to get out of there, as they wanted to work on some shots McGregor would be using against them in later sparring, and he wanted them to come as a surprise.

'Odd,' thought Malignaggi, 'but I'll give them the benefit of the doubt.

'I'm going downstairs complaining to the other sparring partners. "Who does this shit? What the fuck is this?" I'm shadow-boxing downstairs and there's a treadmill. There's nothing else there. I was pissed. So I go to the locker room, get my stuff out, and my phone is always on vibrate. I can hear it through the bag, I can feel the buzzing like mad. It's really going crazy. I had a million messages. My social media was going through the roof. My text messages too. Then I saw it. Conor released photos of me on the canvas. It finally dawned what a piece of shit that guy is. I can't win. He has all the cameras.

'There was the video too, all edited to make him look good. He gives you the punches landed in twelve and then he goes back to eleven so you get the furthest camera view. Nothing lands, but you can't tell that because the straight left is covered by his back. When I re-appear, his hand is behind my neck, that's only because of one thing: he missed. If my head gets hit, it'll whiplash. So he misses, is holding my head down, and from there throws a little smack. I'm pulling away to get my head away and it's a casual slip. If anyone thinks that smack knocked me down ... well, he doesn't hit hard. I pulled back and the momentum is like tug of war: let go of the rope and the other person goes flying.'

In the minivan on the way back to the apartment, Malignaggi fumed. He raged about the place they were put up in, about how they were told they could eat in a healthy restaurant but that many items on the menu weren't allowed due to cost. He told the others he'd been part of relatively small-money training camps but he treated people with respect and it was returned out of decency. And also out of the fact that any time he was preparing, he wanted his sparring partners to be at their very best as that helped him get to his very best. That, after all, was the point of camp.

One fighter he asks not to name but who was part of McGregor's team leaned forward and fist bumped him in agreement. 'The more he makes, the worse he treats everyone and the cheaper he gets,' they said. 'You are right about everything, I understand.'

Malignaggi got out of there. He says he still never took the money owed as he doesn't want it, but in the build up to the fight he saw Attar and wanted a word. 'I was there working for Sky. There was a scrum around Conor, and I tried to get Audie aside and say this isn't cool. Just in private, to talk, as he'd been at that training session. He resisted me, pulling away, he wanted to be among media, as he wants to be famous. Then he says, "No, Paulie." There was tension around the reporters. Conor can't not be the centre of attention, and he gets in my face and then I said, "You've no balls," as I'd told him in camp.

'But there's a saying Conor lives by and must repeat it daily as he's made a living. It's called "Perception is reality." He must know it well. He understands. His entire life is the perception of one thing, when his reality is something else. As long as he can give that great, big lie to the masses, he thinks it's real. When you react to an ass-kicking like he does, always looking for a way to soften the blow and softly quit, then you know. His whole story is a lie. You know he didn't have it as hard as he tries to sell in his story. If you had it that bad, an ass-kicking is not even close to the worst thing. It comes and ends, but the things you went through, you thought you'd never get out of it, they scare you.'

Malignaggi continues on, telling me he's like a wrestling character in his mind, only in a real sport. He tells me others in the MMA community shouldn't look up to him so much either, based on how he hangs around so closely with Dana White. And he tells me that White is notorious for shafting fighters and that includes McGregor. For instance, one contact he has in UFC said that McGregor made €80m from that Mayweather fight, but the UFC made €40m. That may initially not seem like an outrageous split, but remember that this was McGregor's effort and not theirs, indeed it wasn't even their sport.

'If that happened me, I would never speak to you again,' stresses Malignaggi. 'I may be down to a contract, I may have to work with you because of that, but I certainly won't be friends. He hangs out as if White's his buddy. He can't have balls to do that. But he's indulged by those around him. Without a doubt, it's all yes men. All yes men. He does and says whatever he wants. He actually orders them what to say sometimes. I came away from that camp and said everyone there is kissing his ass. I never kissed his ass but never disrespected him. I treated him normal. But when they shake his hand, they are in awe. I spoke and shook hands, man to man. Everyone else speaks, almost asking, "Hey, is that okay?" Tip-toeing. I've been around bigger stars than him, better people than him. I don't give respect based on money you make or fame you have. If I'm guessing right, he didn't like that I didn't put him on a pedestal. I think if you don't do that, he looks at you like a possible enemy. Anyone who doesn't, he hates. It's why he hates Floyd. He kicked his ass, is more famous, is worth more money, and [McGregor] hates that.

'And even Floyd, for all the very real issues, you catch him on his own and he's a normal person. Conor has no sense of reality. He wants to be looked at like a god. But he has to go to bed knowing people fucked him over. If you're God, you aren't bending over. Rich as he is, he'll never be happy, but he'll give you that perception because he lives by that. It rarely ends well. I always tried my best to not let money and fame change me. At times, I'd to tell myself stop treating people this way: you have certain moments caught up in the rush and you say something or do something you shouldn't. But you catch yourself.'

That same week as this was all going on, Mayweather's preparation took place almost exclusively in his strip club. Yet despite that, by the middle rounds, McGregor was the one in trouble out of tiredness more so than an opponent barely trying. By the final bell, all that faked bad blood dissipated.

They'd made their money.

In defeat, McGregor said that was a victory.

The madness had started to lie to him.

* * *

THE MAKING OF THE MADNESS?

It's sad to glance back on now for, in a way, it's like an old couple returning to look at the house they first lived in after marriage, when everything was new and exciting and full of hope. Only they get there and the roof has caved and there are bats in the living room and they realise how much time has passed and that what's gone is gone forever.

Say what you will about McGregor the person, but there was no denying how impressive a fighter he was for a while. Notice the tense though. That Paulie Malignaggi experience and the whole Mayweather farce was proof for any doubters that an era was over in terms of him at his zenith, but for that era to come to an end there had to be a zenith.

There were so many mornings in Ireland where those rooting against him, those who were anywhere between uncomfortable and appalled by his antics, would go online to see what had transpired during an overnight fight, hoping the walls had finally come crumbling down. Time and time again they would be disappointed. Instead what they'd find is a lead photo of him scaling the cage with a tricolor, or one of him standing over a tormented and defeated opponent. The accompanying headline and story would provide details about how dominant he'd been in his latest victory as the rise continued.

Initially, there was either disinterest or scepticism. Even after he knocked out Marcus Brimage in his UFC debut in 2013 in Sweden, there remained a stigma that continued to grab hold of his shoulders and tug him back with all its power, like those exercises when someone hangs from a bungee attached to the athlete. Having stepped up a level from Cage Warriors, any and all experts felt the leap would prove too much. He'd thunder in his fists to win some if he could stay standing tall, but they said he'd lose more often than not as experienced proponents would get him to the ground and for all the improvements he'd made there, this was still throwing a child into the deep end. The way Dana White and the UFC saw it was that, for a while, he'd be a lot of fun and until the act grew stale they'd make money.

How wrong they all were. You only have to look at those he beat, those he swatted away, through the prism of history.

His record is against a mix of those who were at the top of their game already, or those that after losing to him would learn so much that they'd go on to be serious fighters in their own right.

It began with Max Holloway, who wasn't a major name back in August of 2013.

This was a seminal moment for it was then that McGregor's ACL went mid-fight. It meant he'd to go against every instinct and advantage he held, as he took the American to the floor and frankly dominated him there, getting a unanimous decision that never frayed a nerve. There's no doubt that his size was certainly an advantage, as it would continue to be thereafter. For instance, McGregor is arguably more comfortable at 155 pounds, but for this fight he was at 145 pounds, a weight he so often dropped down to, and a weight that allowed him to maintain so much of his power while giving him the size and upper-body strength to have his way. It's a huge sacrifice via saunas, gyms and a lack of food, and a massive disservice to the body for weeks on end, but the sacrifice means the rewards are there come fight night. Only that night in Boston it was also allied to seriously good technique.

It was a first signature win, although the injury and the lack of a highlight-reel knockout meant he'd have to wait a little for another.

When Diego Brandão arrived in Dublin the next summer and McGregor beat him as well, that wasn't seen as too much of a big deal, at least not in fighting terms. Instead this was about the UFC throwing the Irish market a bone and seeing how it would react; dipping a toe to test the water. As it turned out tickets were golden and McGregor kept his end of the deal, not so much by winning, but by selling his cheesy brand of Irishness and pushing open the door open for his bosses to enter. 'We're not here to take part, we're here to take over,' he said as a lingering soundbite. And while not exactly Joycean, his target was more the impressionable fifteen-year-old who was unfortunate enough to be born into the wrong part of a divided society and therefore couldn't see a way forward or a way out. Instead then they hitched themselves to the one guy who had managed to find a way forward and a way out and began to live vicariously through him.

Knowing the numbers were there, the UFC next tested the talent. It was present and correct too.

Dustin Poirier was not so much a past or future contender, he was right there in the moment in September of 2014. A serious operator, yet McGregor decimated him, winning the performance of the night on his Las Vegas debut. The bigger the stage it seemed, the better the act. There was some controversy that the punches raining down at the end were to the top of the head, but even those shouting against the Notorious couldn't but argue this was legitimate in every way.

Four fights in and there was suddenly talk of a title tilt.

This all happened so quickly that is was making some of the more established names uncomfortable, so to slow it the UFC even threw in a roadblock by the name of Dennis Siver. That may seem unfair on the German, but all things were relative beside McGregor at that stage of his career. Calling his opponent a Nazi saw him lose yet more respect but, come the fight, and after another performance of the night, there was no holding the surge anymore.

McGregor-mania was peaking.

José Aldo was scheduled but pulled out injured.

Chad Mendes came in as a replacement for what, as a result, became an interim featherweight title fight in July 2015. And let's break this down, as even for those without a technical interest in the sport, there's something to pay homage to here.

The feeling was that the late call up meant that Mendes would be undercooked and poorly conditioned, and therefore would have to get it done early. He had the tools. A collegiate all-American wrestler, he liked to take it to the floor and once he got there it got interesting and quick. It wasn't that he'd tend to submit his opponents through technical brilliance, instead he'd turn vicious, bludgeoning many out of their consciousness. McGregor did get taken down in that fight and then came the predictable barrage of elbows and fists. He lost the first round. He was losing the second having gone to ground again, but showed enormous heart and pain tolerance.

For all his ego, there was only admiration in that moment.

Mendes had worn himself out in attack, McGregor still had a little in reserve despite being on the wrong end of that attack and rose like a phoenix. It was a rope-a-dope of sorts. That good.

During that bout we got some of the best insight into his cage IQ and his ability to establish good range and pick the right shots. He went with the leg kick often, which is basically a toe poke to the solar plexus that winds someone. In essence it's an investment in your quality, as you believe that it'll take its toll on your opponent later in the fight when you're still hanging about and then you'll capitalise. With round two coming to a close, Mendes was sucking on air and McGregor came roaring and firing off combinations like his very life depended on it. Knockout.

His face may have been sliced open. His good looks may have been damaged.

But he was still smiling through the blood.

He and Holloway may have gone at it on the ground, but that was McGregor's choice due to circumstance. This was out of his control and over and over he got up for more and then more.

It may have been his greatest ever triumph.

Granted, it will never be his most memorable.

12 December, 2015.

The MGM Grand Garden Arena. UFC 194.

UFC World Featherweight Championship.

The rising star of the sport whose mouth made him a curiosity and victories made him a worthy contender, versus José Aldo. The Brazilian was a refined and classy character, the pound-for-pound best mixed martial artist on the planet who hadn't been beaten in a decade. So many like McGregor had come up believing in themselves before and he'd just pushed them back down, reminding them all of their place in his division.

Given Aldo had pulled out of the original bout, it meant there had essentially been two pre-fight tours for this one fight. McGregor got more and more aggressive as the press conferences went on around the world, travelling to Brazil and declaring it his country, and threatening to ride through the shantytowns on horseback while declaring himself the new king after he was done with his opponent. Aldo, everyone presumed, was merely bored of a routine he could barely understand anyway due to the language differences and his non-existent English.

So long had this gone on though that it still got people's attention. Maybe not for the right reasons, maybe purely because of the repetition, but they were looking.

In fact by the time they got around to the actual match up, it was the first McGregor fight that felt like a cultural event in Ireland for those of a certain age. There were tricolours around the shoulders of those on the streets in the capital. A friend recalls how at 3am with the pubs closing, there were gatherings on corners with chants for a guy on the other side of the world that wouldn't be doing his thing for another couple of hours. They were hammered but in good spirits and it brought them together in a way that the national soccer team did at major tournaments or as Steve Collins had done in hope and then glory when beating Benn and Eubank in the 90s.

It felt big and it was big.

To that point it remains right up there with the biggest UFC pay-per-views ever.

While newcomers to this got excited, the weathered fan was busy looking through the strengths and weaknesses. Aldo had it all. Well rounded, extremely fit, ice cool. Besides, for most of the experts, this had come too soon for McGregor, who didn't have the fight-time behind him and thus didn't have the experience and nous. 'I saw it differently,' recalls Gavan Casey, an Irish journalist and expert in boxing and MMA. 'I remember seeing the tactical kicks against Mendes, his intelligence. Also, McGregor kept his power so well at 145, which wasn't natural for him, so that he could dominate opponents who weren't used to that size. On top of that his left hand was as destructive as MMA had ever seen. Aldo wasn't prepared for this machine coming.'

Perhaps most fascinating in the thirteen seconds it lasted was the psychological element. The same one Dave Hill alluded to, but that shouldn't have worked against guys of Aldo's quality. Even today this can be hard to make peace with. The best out there was clearly so wound up by McGregor in the months and moments leading up to it that he threw out everything he'd ever learnt and railed against every instinct when leaving himself wide open. There was no controlled calm, instead there was careless anger. careless anger. Worse for Aldo was the fact that McGregor had told him over and over that this was exactly how he'd win. He'd take a step back at the bell, unleash the left and celebrate.

Thirteen seconds.

Bedlam.

This was seismic beyond MMA as it spilled out into the general sporting landscape.

He was legitimate in the eyes of those who'd desperately tried to detract. Many hated that.

Soon more would hate what it did to him in terms of ever-growing and frankly out-of-control arrogance, although it cemented his massive cult following. He had said he'd clean out the division and told José Aldo how he'd finish his run to the top. And here it was. One of the more iconic moments in Irish sport.

Thereafter? Well how do you follow that act?

There was Nate Diaz, who sources say agreed to fight at 155 but couldn't make it, and McGregor felt so untouchable that he agreed to 170 anyway. From the UFC perspective they'd never had a suitable verbal sparring partner for him, and Diaz was so odd, careless and carefree that it made complete sense. Come fight night though, as Casey recalls, 'Conor often said he was a silverback and he meant it in terms of bigging himself up. I remember saying when watching that bout that he did look like a silverback, but because he was so weighed down by his own physical mass that his body didn't know how to react. Those who had only followed McGregor since his UFC debut for the first time finally saw him as human. He started well but you could see quickly, his body carrying an extra 25 pounds, and the struggle. The way he lost was quite jarring. He was visibly hurting, wobbling on his feet. He looked exhausted, worried, confused, idealess.'

McGregor's script was torn up.

As was the UFC's.

He did come back to win a rematch against Diaz on the scorecards, though it was a highly debatable decision, with many feeling it could and should have gone the other way. However, the pay-per-view sales, standing at around 2.3m, wasn't just a UFC record, but in the top five for combat sports. By then it seemed we were moving into numbers and business and moving away from the guy that seemed like he'd never be stopped. To be fair to him he demanded it be at 170 again, even though that worked against him, as he wanted the first night back and to right a wrong. However, a corner had been turned. Even his last UFC win against Eddie Alvarez in November 2016 seemed like the clock ticking down rather than McGregor carrying on where he left off. That despite the fact that he was back at probably his best weight, 155, his left packed the old punch and his opponent looked like a rabbit in the headlights. He was the UFC's first two-weight champion but if his body hadn't checked out yet, his mind had.

You could sense he was done with it all. You could sense he was bored of it all.

You could sense it was an end.

He'd had his stint as the poster boy for an entire sport.

He'd had his stint as one of the most famous sportspeople on the planet.

Mayweather was about no more than money.

As Marvin Hagler once put it, 'It's tough to get out of bed to do roadwork at 5am when you've been sleeping in silk pyjamas.'

* * *

HERE IN DUBLIN, I'M STILL SITTING WAITING, AS emails come and go but never the ones I want around McGregor and those close to him.

Once more, a message from Audie Attar's assistant reads: 'Mr Attar is travelling and unable to respond to your inquiry. Should anything change I will be in touch.'

Again, I tell the assistant there's no rush and I am more than happy to try and talk to him when he's done. 'We are unable to be of assistance,' comes the reply. 'Thank you.'

An entire industry based on bluster and bullshit.

The problem is there's no place for such nonsense as McGregor moves towards the tail of his career. He needs honesty. He needs reality. He needs real respect. Otherwise, when he's finished, what do you do with all the crazy that at least fighting takes care of for now?

Has Attar ever asked himself this? Is his client's future topping his concerns?

We wonder.

Take Attar's views around xenophobia, racism, and Islamophobia that once saw him react so strongly in a bar and speak so intelligently afterwards. That supposed social conscience doesn't tally with what he's been happy to profit off. He's never spoken out about McGregor calling Dennis Siver a Nazi, or about the dance-for-me boy comments around black people, or about his having a go at Brazilian fighters over their poverty and favelas, or the fact he said he would butcher people in such shantytowns.

Even before the Nurmagomedov loss, Attar described his client's constant ethnic, racial, and religious barbs as mere 'energy and bad blood'. After that, it was a combination of selling those remarks and exploiting his asset some more. 'I said before, there was all this misinformation being thrown about regarding Conor and why he went to New York [when he attacked the bus], and the reality is we almost signed a contract for May for him to fight in Rio. He was already planning on coming back, and I don't think this was a carrot dangled before him that essentially got him back.'

Nowhere in all his yatter was there any condemnation. Indeed, he said of that bus attack, 'It is what it is, so tune in for the real show.' You may not like or agree with Malignaggi, but this certainly fits into the category of yes men and money at any and all cost. A theory that the

UFC doesn't just survive on but thrives off, all while putting fighters down the priority list.

In such a way, McGregor getting to do what he wants isn't good for him, but it is good for balance sheets. As the UFC so often see it, be it around physical or mental health, it's nothing ventured around wellbeing, nothing gained in terms of the sales.

If McGregor and UFC's sales pitch is to make the same type of vile remarks that once rightly upset Attar so much back in his university years, then that's the fundamental problem with marketing. Rules and attitudes change depending on profits. That means massive hypocrisy.

As for McGregor, he ought to have his own questions for his agent. Or maybe he's already asked and maybe the answer is already satisfactory. But there's no sporting sphere better than combat sports for fallen heroes and burnt-out stars. Joe Louis ended up as a greeter in Caesar's Palace. Rocky Lockridge lived on the streets. Leon Spinks blew his fortune mostly on drugs. Iran Barkley was in a halfway house trying to get back on his feet. Wilfredo Benitez sits in a wheelchair waiting for the next social welfare cheque. Felix Trinidad's advisors wasted $63m on government bonds that were mere junk. Tommy Hearns auctioned his life's possessions away to pay tax. Mike Tyson was Mike Tyson.

That's the danger here: is it all aboard the gravy train with McGregor? Does his agent show real respect which means he doesn't hand out free respect? Can he be sure bills are paid and he's being set up for the future? As an example, LeBron James's media manager helped turn Arnold Schwarzenegger from an action star to governor of California, such was the level of respect and talent. We don't know about Attar, though, as his client list consists of McGregor, some smaller MMA fighters, and a handful of have-beens or never-will-bes from elsewhere.

'Never doubt your client's own confidence in what they want to do,' Attar said previously. 'Going back to when I was a young athlete, that was my belief. You couldn't tell me any different. To compete at that level, you gotta have that self-belief. You gotta have that conviction in your own dreams. If that's really what you want, you need to work for it. Conor saying, "I'm going to win two belts," that's big. If he's going to believe, I'm going to believe. So I think what's interesting is in my life and in my company [is that] you don't always attract the right people. The ones who stick around, they gravitate to each other for the right reasons. You stay with each other for performance and good business, but you gravitate to each other because you think the same way … I've never once told him an idea of his was crazy.'

If only he had, there'd be more method and less madness.

Little wonder no one close to McGregor wants to talk.

When image is everything, this truth becomes more dangerous still.

CHAPTER 9

VERTIGO

Beating his wings harder and harder, Icarus soared up into the sky and out over the Aegean Sea. It was hard to believe it but the plan had worked. For here he was now, flying alongside his father, Daedalus, as they left the island of Crete behind them and travelled on towards their freedom. Icarus glanced over at his father and grinned.

'Come along, Father,' he shouted, over the sound of the wind rushing past them.

'Smile, we've done it, we've escaped and we're free.'

'When my feet are back on solid ground and that island is many, many miles behind us, then you will see me smile,' Daedalus yelled back. 'Now, keep your mind on what we have *to do and remember, not too high, not too close to the sun.'*

It's Wednesday.

The Las Vegas sun is beating down outside.

Three days to fight night, and the open workouts are taking place in the MGM's Park Theater.

Conor McGregor is late.

He's always late.

It's his thing, like some impressive trick he's mastered, worthy of so much pride as to be repeated ad nauseam. To those who have gathered in the auditorium it is impressive, though. This is part of the act that makes him unique. The big screens show him arriving in the car park. Then strutting into the building. Then he comes on stage.

There's a roar every time, each one bigger than the last.

No sooner is he in front of us than he's gone again. On this occasion, it's a change of clothes that's required, from designer suit to gym apparel. This is not to the baying crowd's liking, though, as they need a bigger dose of their drug, a quick hit not being enough. 'Does he *need* fucking Gucci?' snaps a guy pressed against a steel rail. Minutes later, his anger is replaced by forgiveness as McGregor returns in his workout gear, with his young son barely walking by his side.

His personal photographer takes a few snaps of them together for some family album they can all look at down the line. This is optimistic, I think, but then there's no harm in optimism.

Many in the crowd aren't thinking, though.

'Nurmagomedov is a cunt,' one person shouts.

'He's a fucking wanker,' screams another.

'That Dagestani bastard,' comes from the back.

'You'll make him your bitch,' comes from the front.

And so it goes on as the crowd whip themselves into the most macho frenzy they can concoct. Next up, they're calling Khabib 'a faggot'. It's baffling. Here they are in the most homoerotic of settings, staring open mouthed at a ripped man in the tightest pair of ball-clinging briefs rolling around on the floor before getting onto all fours and rolling some more. And yet to them, the suggestion of homosexuality is an insult.

It's one more contradiction, one more insight into the muddled mindset of the mob.

As for an insight into McGregor, that comes when he gets back on two feet and starts to work on his striking. His forte seemingly, but he is outright slow. The shots are heavy for sure, and there is the telltale tear of power as he hits leather. But it's like a lad throwing punches in a nightclub brawl. One. Break. Reload. Then two.

It's not so much impressive as it is a worry.

Those two years out have clearly seen the messages coming from the brain slow as they make their way through the neck and tell his arms to strike again. He knows what he wants to do, but his body fights back.

Many of the other journalists don't take this in. Instead, they feel honoured to be in his presence. They don't watch his movement but turn their backs to get a selfie, a brag about being so close to someone they are supposed to be analysing objectively. This press pack is a part of the present and very much the future of media, as they all have cameras rather than notepads, with the need for everything to be visual and instant. Fading is the era of some thought-out reflection as it will be too late to market. They are writing for the fans almost as fans, rather than coldly as journalists.

The crowd isn't as big given the time of year, as Irish kids with J1 visas fill out summer events but have left before this came around. A rare slip on the UFC's part, although the company are probably just glad to get McGregor back as they wring a nearly dried-out towel for the last few drops. But there's enough to make a racket and to satisfy an ego.

Done with a fairly flabby workout, McGregor's new job takes over.

Marketing. Lately, his purpose has become various ads for his whiskey brand Proper 12. Named after the Dublin 12 area where Crumlin is located, it's supposed to be a hat-tip to where he came from. His energy and his shameless sales at every turn are supposedly carrying it, and it's an investment in whatever future he has. It's not just online: sit-down interviews see him grasping a bottle and talking over questions about MMA and various fights, as his learned-off spiel about the quality of the product fills the mics. It's as if he's more caught up in this than the sport, as if it gives him a long-lost thrill.

So here and now, he stands on the edge of the stage with his arms outstretched, somewhere between a conductor and a priest, riling up his worshipers.

Chants of 'Fuck the Jameson Brothers' grow loud, referring to what he sees as a competitor in the whiskey marketplace, and therefore his fans see as a competitor too.

To look at him, he's untouchable.

To look at him, he's Icarus.

What's it like to stand on that stage, though?

What's it like to soar so high?

* * *

BACK IN 1956, IN THE JOURNAL PSYCHIATRY, Donald Horton and Richard Wohl wrote 'Mass Communication and Para-Social Interaction: Observations on Intimacy at a Distance'.

The introduction reads, 'One of the striking characteristics of the new mass media – radio, television, and the movies – is that they give the illusion of a face-to-face relationship with the performer. The conditions of response to the performer are analogous to those in a primary group. The most remote and illustrious men are met as if they were in the circle of one's peers; the same is true of a character in a story who comes to life in these media in an especially vivid and arresting way. We propose to call this seeming face-to-face relationship between spectator and performer a para-social relationship.' In the study, the duo added of the fans:

> The audience is expected to accept the situation defined by the programme format as credible, and to concede as 'natural' the rules and conventions governing the actions performed and the values realized. It should play the role of the loved one to the persona's lover; the admiring dependent to his father-surrogate; the earnest citizen to his fearless opponent of political evils. It is expected to benefit by his wisdom, reflect on his advice, sympathize with him in his difficulties, forgive his mistakes, buy the products that he recommends, and keep his sponsor informed of the esteem in which he is held... The audience is expected to contribute to the illusion by believing in it, and by rewarding the persona's 'sincerity' with 'loyalty'. The audience is entreated to assume a sense of personal obligation to the performer, to help him in his struggle for 'success' if he is 'on the way up', or to maintain his success if he has already won it. 'Success' in show business is itself a theme which is prominently exploited in this kind of propaganda. It forms the basis of many movies; it appears often in the patter of the leading comedians and in the exhortations of MC's; it dominates the so-called amateur hours and talent shows; and it is subject to frequent comment in interviews with 'show people'.

Consider that in terms of the fan, but also consider what it does to the star. Only few do. In fact, despite this bloated era of worship, only two or three serious studies have ever been done around how fame changes someone's psyche, the most thorough published in 1989, long before social media came along and made many aspects redundant.

What experts do say is that celebrity forces people to see themselves objectively, through the eyes of others, and that a human is not designed to handle that. It means we may see McGregor as the predator, be that as a fighter or, more recently, as a marketing object hoovering up any and all profit. What if he's merely our prey, though?

The study was still more accurate when it noted of the celebrity rather than the star, 'Beyond the coaching of specific attitudes towards personae, a general propaganda on their behalf flows from the performers themselves, their press agents, and the mass communication industry. Its major theme is that the performer should be loved and admired. Every attempt possible is made to strengthen the illusion of reciprocity and rapport in order to offset the inherent impersonality of the media themselves. The jargon of show business teems with special terms for the mysterious ingredients of such rapport: ideally, a performer should have 'heart,' should be 'sincere'; his performance should be 'real' and 'warm'. The publicity campaigns built around successful performers continually emphasize the sympathetic image which, it is hoped, the audience is perceiving and developing.'

The characteristics of what people want and therefore get may have changed from real and warm, but with McGregor, and many more, the fundamental idea remains the same.

It can be hard to see that through the colour and noise here and now. Outside the auditorium and at the bar, instead of considering this, there's a flurry of activity, with fans wanting beer and talking about what he'll do to Nurmagomedov, while media are looking for some hot take around what we've seen before, over and over. It's hardly surprising but they are missing out. Look past this bluster and it's been remarkable to see such a theory play out around a kid from Crumlin on a Vegas stage.

William Todd Schultz is a professor of psychology at Pacific University, who has been looking at the issue of being a celebrity and the damage that can and is doing, even in the very early stages of this new world. He has mostly studied artists rather than the wider field of celebrity, but his thoughts still hold true across that wider spectrum. 'I think for some people, because of what their personality is like and what their life history is like, they can manage fame – without experiencing it as a trauma,' he explains. 'They almost seem to enjoy it, they aren't completely unraveled by it. But then there are other people who, for a complicated combination of reasons, find fame to be an overwhelming experience that ends up being traumatic and can end up being potentially disastrous, depending on how it plays out. Some people have a vulnerable, fragile self-image to begin with and they achieve fame solely because of their talents. One reason that they have those talents is just because they are sort of sensitive, perceptive people. That feeds into and strengthens the art they make. It makes captivating art. But the same things that make them good artists make them vulnerable to fame. So they just are less equipped to deal with the scrutiny and constant reactions to everything they are doing, and to people telling them who they are from a distance. People who are strangers and fans who don't know them. So it starts to mess with their sense of self. You're this vulnerable person who goes into the world. You go out and make art and you think to begin with you'd like to be famous, but you'd really like people to appreciate the art you make, to listen to your songs or read your books or poetry or whatever. You've this abstract sense of fame, but it's not fame you are after.

'You want to express yourself, but then it arrives and this thing you thought you wanted, you find has a lot of negative aspects too. And lately, social media's addition can be overwhelming. Through no choice, you are subject to constant scrutiny by people. In this day and age, they can say whatever they want about you all the time, and in this day and age, you probably have to develop a thick skin where you don't have to pay attention to it or ignore it if you can, but even that is hard to do, as it's your career and you've to keep track of what people are saying. In the old days, you'd do whatever you did and there'd be newspapers, but you wouldn't be subject to this constant onslaught of people who for bizarre reasons hate you or, for equally bizarre reasons, love you, and they become obsessed with you through that and incorporate you into their fantasies. Either option isn't good for you. It creates crazy and you have then to contend with that all the time.'

If the techniques and technology to exploit such parasocial relationships had years to develop, then has there been a more perfect sporting example than McGregor? Probably not, and that's partly his own fault, even if he didn't know what path he was traipsing down, because he was always unable to see around the next bend until he was there.

He ought to be niche due to MMA's position in the spectrum, but he's huge in a wider sense regardless of his sport. On top of that, he's either adored or vilified, with no one ever sitting on the fence. And despite all that, so few actually know him or the affect of this adoration, other than the chaos that seeps beyond the control of public relations and makes its way into gossip columns and news. With him, it's as if he held up a mask one day not so long ago, but if he were to ever remove the mask, there'd be nothing left behind it. As if his existence has become a creation of those that follow him. As if he's surrendered control through identification.

'If you've a secure sense of self, which some people have, you can navigate that and take it in your stride and not be completely freaked out,' Schultz continues. 'But if you're already an insecure person – and it's not like security and confidence and self assertion are prerequisite for fame – it just heightens it. One thing that happens, you feel you've to live up to this image in other people's minds and it's not really an image you identify with or who you are. But all these people are expecting you to be x, y or z and you get seduced into a role that others have foisted on you. That gradually comes to define you. A crazy guy. A bad girl. You feel like even though part of you knows it's wrong, it feels like you have to play out this set of expectations people have about you.

'Some of the time, you feel false and fraudulent but part of you can't stop being that, as that's what people think you are and that's what your fame depends on. We all end up playing a role in life, but their role becomes one-dimensional in the mind of the public, and if they don't perform as is expected, the public is disappointed when the reality is that's not even who they are. You do lose track of who the original you is. You can get very confused about who you are.

'This false self pulverises the original true self, and to survive it you have to end up finding a way to get strong enough to reject the false self and embrace the true self crushed into the background for many years. In a lot of cases, you probably end up deeply confused. Look at Britney Spears and people like that. I'm sure it gets to a point where they don't know who they are anymore. There are some who avoid this but they tended to have had a good childhood, strong support, friends they can trust. Others are neurotic, fragile, and this supersaturated world of people laying in on you all the time, that ends up being really difficult.'

Which one sounds like McGregor to you?

That's rhetorical and comes back to the self-doubt before fame, the support network that warned him against even trying to make it in MMA, and the speed with which all of this happened, meaning there was never time for preparation or planning.

'Some get addicted just because it fills them up and makes them feel loved and adored,' Schultz says. 'They kind of depend on fans and media to make them feel good about themselves, and that's a dangerous thing as it's so fickle. One day they love you ...' There are many instances of this in McGregor's combat sports world. There are many instances of it out across the sporting landscape. But when thinking of his life, one story always comes to mind.

It's that of Brian Bosworth, the 1980s American football linebacker.

* * *

BRIAN KEITH BOSWORTH FEATURED IN THE BRILLIANT ESPN *30 for 30* documentary *Brian and the Boz.*

Even the introduction by director Thaddeus Matula screams a stunning crossover as he explains that the tale is 'the creation of the modern athlete and the high cost that had on the human being behind that superhero, larger-than-life creation ... In this film, we see a metamorphosis as he sheds his image of what he thought Brian was supposed to be, and what everybody wanted the Boz to be, to find who he is somewhere in the middle.'

His ghost writer Rick Reilly said, 'I never met an athlete who could market himself better.'

Bosworth himself said, 'If you tell me I can't do something, I'm going to go and do it,' before adding at the start, 'I'm gonna come across as a psychological mess in this, you know that?'

The film then follows him and his son Max to a storage unit in Texas, where they go through what his late father kept in terms of career memorabilia.

Consider all of the following in terms of McGregor as well.

Bosworth could never satisfy his old man who, not even his coach in school, made him run laps after practice. It was a trigger that left all kinds of insecurity in the person and all kinds of doubt in the athlete. The only remedy was to play with fear manifested as rage, to go at full speed even when it didn't make sense, as it saw him throw self-regard away. He was a brilliant athlete, with both size and speed allied to technique and aggression, who started to see himself as more of a product than a person to the point he was always for sale. He was a man for his time and place: the 1980s were made for loud music and outrageous outfits and big hair. He was a being who couldn't stop the cameras coming, who had to say something with shock value every time he spoke, and who feared the noise would go quiet. He was flawed due to the need for attention that mostly came from kids who saw him as a superhero, while those around him could only see the turmoil. He had an agent come along and push it further to the point that season previews in papers led with pictures of him lying in front of a Corvette, and the copy spoke of 'sex, drugs and college football'. He was the villain. It's what drives ratings, which in turn makes money.

Conor or Brian?

The Notorious or the Boz?

If anything, Bosworth should be a warning for McGregor. Blow too much air into a balloon and the inevitable happens. Having been banned from the 1987 Orange Bowl for steroid use, and warned by his coach not to do anything that took away from the efforts of those playing, he showed up on the sideline with a T-shirt that screamed for attention. On it, the acronym NCAA spelled out 'National Communists Against Athletes', with the finishing touch being 'Welcome to Russia.' It saw him booted from Oklahoma and welcomed into the NFL.

'In a matter of ten seconds, I undid everything good,' Bosworth says. 'That shirt is the reason that I fell so hard. This is something I'm not proud of. You can always make a statement about how you feel in the right way, or you can say it the wrong way. I know you think it's funny, but this is not who I am, and I've apologised to my teammates and my school and my coach because of this. It was not necessary. If there's one thing I could take back, I'd take this back. Sometimes, it's good to have reminders of the mistakes you make. I'll keep it. But I'd rather you not idolise it.'

It wasn't any better in the NFL. He wrote to a list of teams telling them not to draft him as they weren't worthy, and when Seattle did, he refused to play. That is until they presented him with the biggest contract in the franchise's history. He arrived to his first training session in a helicopter, alienated the dressing room, called out John Elway to the point where all the Denver Broncos fans bought T-shirts that said 'Ban the Boz' not knowing it was Bosworth's own company that had had them printed. He wasn't finished with his old college, either. In his autobiography, which came across as him wanting you to think he was the animal that marketing portrayed, he bemoaned a drug culture and gun culture at the university. He caused an outrage and lost friends for life. 'That is when the Boz went Broadway,' he explained. 'This isn't real anymore, this is scripted reality.'

Injured young, he slipped into a depression for years and only recently managed to escape. That's what can happen when what drives you is so dark. Meanwhile, looking at a photo from his heyday, he commented: 'You see awesome, I see lost. It's people thinking you're more than you are. I'm just a football player.'

What does McGregor see when he looks at himself in a photo?

After the Notorious is done with him, will Conor be able to live a normal life?

Maybe some day, McGregor and his son will go to a storage locker. Maybe some day, they'll laugh at the picture of his boy with him on stage at this open workout here in Vegas. Maybe it'll all be okay. But this isn't the fantasy he exists in right now, and not all endings like Bosworth's are happy.

With a whoop of excitement, he soared up and up, gliding around the sky, zooming back down towards his father and then up again, up, up, up towards the dazzling sun.

'Icarus, not too high, not too close to the sun,' his father

screamed in desperation. 'The wax on your wings will melt. Stay close to me and stay low.'

But his words fell on deaf ears. The boy continued to soar up into the bright blue sky, edging nearer and nearer to the sun and, as Daedalus flew along below him, he saw a bright white feather flutter through the sky and, looking up, watched in horror as more and more feathers detached themselves from his son's wings.

He watched in despair as his son began to lose height and his despair turned to total anguish as he heard the terrified cry from his son, as he tumbled and spun past him towards the sea below. It took only seconds, but it seemed like a lifetime, as Daedalus saw his son plummet through the sky with increasing speed to hit the waters below with a resounding splash.

Conor McGregor began his Mixed Martial Arts Career in 2008 with a victory over Gary Morris, but it wasn't until April 2013 he made his UFC debut, defeating Marcus Brimage in Stockholm. Here he stares into the camera at a press conference ahead of his second UFC bout, this time against Max Holloway. [InPho]

Right from the start, it seemed that he had the press eating out of his hand. [InPho]

There was plenty of anticipation for the fight against Holloway in Boston, which was to be broadcast live on Setanta Sports in Ireland. [Sportsfile]

McGregor's family made the trip to watch his first fight in a country he would become very familiar with. His father Tony (left) was once against his son pursuing a career in the sport but is now a near constant presence ringside. [Getty]

McGregor's second UFC win was a seminal moment in his career, coming despite the fact that he tore his Anterior Cruciate Ligament halfway through the bout. [Getty]

With news of McGregor spreading like wildfire, the 02 in Dublin was packed for his home UFC debut against Diego Brandão, another victory achieved by TKO. [Getty]

McGregor's talent for the sport was obvious, and it didn't take long for UFC's Dana White to see he had a talent for driving profits as well. Ahead of the McGregor's first fight in Las Vegas, the promoter keeps him and Dustin Poirier at arm's length. [Getty]

White has long been the driving force behind UFC and the circus it brings with it – in 2001 he was installed as the company's president after it was purchased by the Fertitta Brothers. It was Dana that told the pair it was for sale, and here he is pictured in between Frank and Lorenzo in London. [Getty]

At the peak of his powers, McGregor works out in the gym ahead of his fight with Dennis Siver in January 2015. Cameras capture the action in the background. [Getty]

McGregor is congratulated by his opponent Chad Mendes in the aftermath of victory in Las Vegas in July 2015. Blood stains the canvas. [Getty]

After six straight victories, McGregor's opponent for the unification of the featherweight division was José Aldo. White announced in the build-up that UFC had spent more on this fight than any in its history, and so naturally it was left to the fighters to show how much they hated each other ahead of battle. [Getty]

It was a big moment for the Crumlin-born fighter, whose career had been working up to this point. Prior to the fight, his coach and father figure John Kavanagh makes sure he is prepared properly. [Getty]

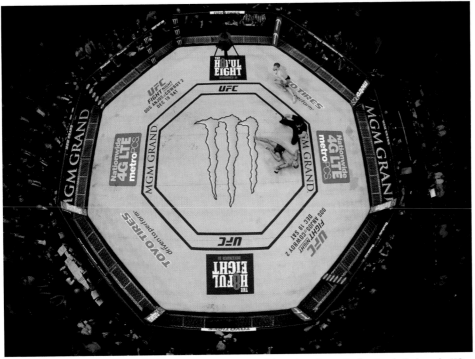

The moment when victory becomes a reality for McGregor is captured from above. It was the first time he had won by KO in his UFC career, and it took him just thirteen seconds to destroy the seemingly untouchable Aldo. A legend had been created. [Getty]

Following the victory, he takes a moment to soak in the atmosphere of the MGM Grand. [Getty]

Success mixed with marketability inevitably leads to stardom. In December 2015, as his popularity continued to soar, McGregor appeared on Jimmy Kimmel live. [Getty]

Though McGregor would suffer his first defeat in UFC at the hands of Nate Diaz in March of 2016, the party continued. In July 2016, he was a guest at Jennifer Lopez's birthday party and met Cristiano Ronaldo, no stranger to the limelight either. [Getty]

Still prepared to put in the hard yards, McGregor returns to the gym, his sanctuary and salvation, ahead of a rematch with Diaz in August 2016, a bout he would win. [Getty]

Ahead of his fighting debut in New York against Eddie Alvarez, McGregor returns to Straight Blast Gym, the venue where he learnt to hone his craft under John Kavanagh, for a training session. A sign reminds visitors – and perhaps McGregor himself – of the rules upon entry. [Getty]

Overleaf: Following his victory over Alvarez, McGregor's ego told him that he could take on the undefeated boxer Floyd Mayweather – in a boxing contest. Titled 'The Money Fight', it was a contest designed to generate income and publicity rather than a serious battle. [Getty]

Six months on from the Alvarez victory, McGregor makes himself noticed at the Grand National in Aintree. It is the beginning of a five-day session on Merseyside which would generate all sorts of headlines for the wrong reasons. [PA]

Despite McGregor's loss to Mayweather, everyone was a winner, especially Lorenzo Fertitta (left) and Dana White (right). [Getty]

'His entire life is the perception of one thing, when the reality is something else.' Former world welterweight champion Paulie Malignaggi was drafted to help McGregor prepare for the fight, but soon realised what a farce the whole thing was. [Getty]

McGregor poses with Russian president Vladimir Putin during the 2018 World Cup clash between France and Croatia. Putin would later meet with McGregor's next opponent, Khabib Nurmagomedov, and refused to condemn the violence from Khabib's backroom team that followed the pair's fight. [Getty]

Just eleven days after meeting Putin, McGregor appears in the New York Supreme Court after being charged with multiple counts of assault and criminal mischief after attacking a bus filled with UFC fighters at the Barclays Centre. He pleaded guilty to a lesser charge of disorderly conduct and was handed a punishment of five days' community service. [Getty]

Shortly before taking a swing at his opponent on stage, McGregor looks out at his adoring fans at the weigh-in for his fight with Khabib Nurmagomedov. [Getty]

Yet despite all the abuse, xenophobia and histrionics, Nurmagomedov was far too good for his opponent on the night. To this day, it remains McGregor's last fight in UFC. [Getty]

McGregor and his son, Conor Jack McGregor Jr., on the field prior to Super Bowl LIII in Atlanta, February 2019. [Getty]

CHAPTER 10

FAME

A TRUE STORY. AND, FRANKLY, AN EMBARRASSING one for all concerned.

For a little while, as strange as it may seem, Conor McGregor put his rise down to something other than himself. When he was younger, struggling along with life and MMA, and not yet filled with belief, it wouldn't have been hard to view him as a lost soul. He was the square peg when society had laid out only round holes. Fit in or get out.

His sister Erin could see this and, having read a book called *The Secret* by Rhonda Byrne, she passed it on into the next room. Conor was hugely sceptical but once, after a particularly crappy day, he gave in and had a look. Learning it had been adapted into a film, he and his girlfriend Dee got hold of the DVD. 'Even when I first watched it,

I was like, "This is bullshit,"' he said. 'But then something clicked for me. We would be driving to the shop and visualising the exact car park space. And then we'd be able to get it every time.'

Let's be frank. His first opinion was spot on. 'Bullshit' is a great word to describe the book.

Found amongst the self-help genre, a cursory glance immediately raises the question: how can it be self-help when its premise is based on someone else helping you? Indeed, the whole notion of self-help is farcical, suggesting as it does that you can do it yourself, in which case you surely don't need any help to begin with.

Aside from trying to be pedantic and accurate, though, what's between the covers can be described as anything from vacuous pap to dangerous, as the premise is that what you imagine will happen. It's not even original: this idea of the 'law of attraction', as Byrne called it, goes back to a 1903 book called *As a Man Thinketh*. One passage reads: 'The soul attracts that which it secretly harbors, that which it loves, and also that which it fears. It reaches the height of its cherished aspirations. It falls to the level of its unchastened desires – and circumstances are the means by which the soul receives its own.'

Rhonda Byrne is an Australian television producer, but what McGregor read had her coming across as an out-and-out charlatan. The title comes from the idea that there's some secret that successful people have kept largely hidden, and that it's the reason for their success, passed on to a select few. These people included, according to Byrne's imagination, Buddha, Aristotle, Plato, Isaac Newton, Martin Luther King Jr, Carl Jung, Henry Ford, Ralph Waldo Emerson, Thomas Edison, Albert Einstein, Winston Churchill, Andrew Carnegie, Joseph Campbell, Alexander Graham Bell, and Beethoven. But worse is what it tries to get ordinary people to buy into. If you're a cancer sufferer, according to such sentiments, you can positively think yourself better.

The flip-side, of course, is that if, say, you're a rape victim, that's on you as well, since your thoughts caused you to be violated.

But that didn't matter at the time, for such logic flew in the face of what was trendy back then, and thus the book quickly became a bestseller. Celebrities pushed it and credited it for getting them to the top. It even got Oprah's seal of approval as she told a generation what to read.

All in all, it was one more summation of the age we live in.

While McGregor still touts it as life-changing though, here's a question for him. Since his thinking rather than his own manic dedication and skill got him to this sporting zenith and remarkable life, is his thinking also responsible for the bad and the baggage that has come along with his success? Because let's not pretend being a champion comes on its own. Fame is attached.

Be careful what you wish for.

There's a moment in the 2017 McGregor documentary that somehow made it past his checks and screening. In fact, it was about the only moment outside of his training where we got to peer into the real world he inhabits. The scene is a Las Vegas car park after the weigh-in: as he heads for his vehicle, McGregor is spotted by a horde of fans. Suddenly, they make their way towards him like zombies, and he panics.

No doubt the timing is bad, as for any fighter at that point all you want is food and drink, alone in a hotel room, in order to regain fluids and body mass. But with the door locked and him unable to get in, he snaps at his team. He doesn't want these fans.

Many famous people hate being famous for the most part and McGregor certainly doesn't seem so different in that regard. That's the problem with being a celebrity: it's a bell you can't unring.

* * *

DUBLIN DOESN'T HELP, FOR ITS SMALL SIZE MEANS everything is magnified.

Certainly, this town ain't big enough for the both of him, the committed athlete and the outrageous superstar.

Kenneth Egan knows that, even though he's relatively small-time next to McGregor. From Clondalkin, another working-class area a few miles from Crumlin, he became big news locally when he brought home a silver medal in boxing from the 2008 Olympics. He had the good looks and a goofy charm to go with the relative sporting success, meaning that, for a brief stint, everyone around here wanted a piece of him.

Recently, he got round to watching that McGregor film, and the first thing that struck him was the training. 'Now I'm split, for I don't know how difficult it is to make it in that sport,' he says, referring to the narrow base of the pyramid in MMA due to small popularity and participation on a global scale. 'It's not like Olympic boxing – a hundred years, massive numbers, huge competition. But that aside, his work ethic and how he disciplined himself when in his training camp, the work he puts into himself physically and mentally, is second to none. Everything he does is for his craft and he really studies it. I have to say, I wish I had ten percent of his discipline. It is savage. Maybe that's changed today, but back then, he was at the highest level and it was easy to see why. The shape he gets himself in, even making weight, it's bloody hard and he has to pull off crazy amounts of weight. The sacrifice and discipline and determination, and he has all that. Or had it.'

But that isn't what I came to talk to him about. Instead, I'm curious as to what happens when the training and fighting ends. His own experience was one that saw him gobbled up by Dublin. Coming home with that medal, he was the toast of every tabloid, the pride of every party, always smiling and seemingly living the high life. Except he couldn't handle it and eventually turned to drink. An alcoholic, at one stage he skipped boxing and town and disappeared to New York in his pomp without telling anyone. A country wondered where he was but he'd turned off his phone. The media were in a race to find out what happened him and to get the first quote, meanwhile all he wanted was to be left alone for a little while with his thoughts and with a pint.

Multiply that by thousands and you get nearer to the world in which McGregor exists.

'That fame, I wouldn't wish it on my worst enemy, on no one,' Egan admits. 'People look at you differently and you can see that. They stare at you a bit longer. I thought they thought I was immortal, that I was something different. And I wasn't, I was still the same person. I'd just achieved something in sport. It made me feel a bit different then. "Why do they want to talk to me or want photo after photo after photo?" It's very strange and surreal, and it goes from exciting to a pain very fast. When I got home from the Games, I saw my Ma in the airport, and then saw the lads in the club and there was an open-top bus to the local pub. I would have been happy for it to stop then, but it was constant. Almost uncomfortable. I obviously started drinking and you do that to escape, but that just brings on more shit, because obviously you are doing that in public and your guard comes way down. You're trying to escape the person you are by engaging in that. All you want to be is normal again, but you can't go back when everyone wants a piece of you.

'It's not just me, it is your family. It happens so quick. As soon as I won my quarter-final, it's the medal stages, and the house got bombarded and it's not what we are used to around here. This estate doesn't get attention. My Dad had to come home early from work because my Mam couldn't handle everyone trying to push their way in, setting up tripods, making themselves feel at home. That was all because of me and I knew nothing about that, because I was away just being a boxer. Even my brothers [were] being approached by people to find out where I was that time I went to New York, to try and get a story. It snowballs. They all go from celebrating [you] to looking for dirt. And I wasn't emotionally mature, I was in that bubble straight away and I didn't know what real life was. Nothing about mortgages or bills or being a good person. Not even that, a normal person.

'I ended up drinking in town, that never happened before. Coppers, Krystle, then Lillie's. That's not me. I feel uncomfortable in these fancy places, but all of a sudden, I could walk in and not get asked for ID, and you get a kick out of people seeing you and their faces change. You see it and use it to your advantage. It's like magic. At times, I thought this was great, but there's a lot of people exploiting you. You get hangers-on as well. I suppose I was using them as much as they were using me, too. I was trying to get back into the gym, and the expectation was there and I struggled with that. That was a big weight. People build you up. That was added pressure; I was drinking and I did underperform. So I can't imagine what it's like for Conor. If only we saw more of that dedication. I don't know who he hangs around with, but there's always the talk of that gang. Does he need to be associating with these people as a high-performing athlete?'

He's far from alone in finding fame a hidden trap within sporting success.

Some are just lucky or wise enough to give it a wider berth.

By 2012, before McGregor had so much as made his UFC debut, Katie Taylor became one of Ireland's biggest stars when she won gold at the London Games. 'I kind of got overwhelmed by it all,' she said later on. 'I was in my own little bubble after London, and I didn't realise how big it was back home. And it hit me when I was home, and I just needed to get away from it for a while.'

Since going pro, she's remained one of the bigger names in Irish sport, her record staying perfect while unifying the world titles. But knowing what was coming, she retreated to rural Connecticut. In an interview with *Ring Magazine*, she suggested that 'there's something freeing about that. I love the fact that I'm anonymous over here and I can go for walks and stuff like that. I definitely live a very quiet life when I'm at home in Ireland as well, but I do love that I can just be myself over here.' Indeed, while her Manchester ROCs gym has a banner for the best and brightest who train in it, when asked why hers was absent, she replied, 'I don't want a banner.'

Contrast that attitude with McGregor.

Others have found more troublesome ways to escape what they inadvertently created, burning down the house to get the flies from the kitchen. From Wales rugby legend Barry John, who got out of the game early and turned to drink; to former LA Raiders quarterback Todd Marinovich, who found sanctuary in drugs. From wild and beloved darts great Jocky Wilson, who hid out across his remaining years in a Scottish council house, broke and with diabetes, refusing the many requests from media to tell his remarkable story; to one of sport's biggest geniuses in snooker player Ronnie O'Sullivan, who worked as a volunteer on a pig farm for a year to rediscover quiet.

Too often they, like McGregor, tied their self-worth to their antics as well as their athletic prowess.

For McGregor, being the Notorious means that for many he's obnoxious and unliked, but being Conor means he's nothing. Everything has to be outrageous, and from that there can be no way out. Deep down, is he still the lad from Crumlin who wasn't good enough? Does he feel the need to rail against the doubters, including himself, in every moment?

Perhaps for McGregor, this lifestyle is a jail the persona craves but the person hates. It's hard to tell, but looking at him in that very real moment in the car park, it's like being at sea in a storm: all you can do is batten down the hatches, bring down the sail, and see what's left come morning. McGregor remains caught up in that violent episode.

Floyd Landis knows a thing or two about this side of fame and infamy. When the cyclist had his Tour de France title stripped for doping, he turned whistleblower, lost everything including his mind, and retreated to a cabin in the California wilderness. There, he started each day with tablets washed down with whiskey, in the hope of ending the pain. He'd later re-emerge as one of the most insightful sportspeople of all.

We've talked before about everything from his life to his career to his doping to the position of those that simply tell the truth in a rancid sporting landscape. But delving into this idea of celebrity and its costs excites him. 'Forget all the other stuff,' Landis says. 'This is one we got to get into. This is interesting.'

Even though his level of fame may not have been near that of McGregor either, the level of hatred was up there. When he was on the receiving end, social media was in its infancy, with most online talk splattered below reports and articles, on newspaper sites, as well as on the early blogs that began to give everyone and anyone a voice. He didn't even have real time to bask in that 2006 Tour de France win when a test result came back positive and he was suddenly thrown onto the pile of those despised.

Today, he's the rare sort of ex-athlete who will allow you to sit back and let the cogs of the tape recorder roll and roll.

'I've spent a lot of time thinking about it, obviously, because I lived through it,' he explains of being the centre of attention. 'Now it's even worse: everyone has a place to say what they want, and it's rarely anything positive. But when you are in the middle of it and it's directed at you, I guess that depends on your personality, but for most, you want to prove them wrong and to argue and to fight, but there's nothing you can do. I used to read these comments and my reaction was all over the place. It used to get me more mad than anything, seeing people talk about how great the anti-doping agencies were, when the whole thing was a fucking fraud through and through. It was hypocrisy. Double standards. You want to fight that. You want to shout sense at people.'

Only he couldn't.

Recently mountain biking in Oregon where he now runs a marijuana business, a burst tire forced him to ask the driver of a pick-up truck for a lift back into town. As they got moving, the driver told him that he'd spotted him and wasn't going to say anything but since he was sitting beside him, he might as well be honest. "Floyd, I saw you over there and it made me think I was one of those guys on the internet that went way overboard, and I guess I deserve this. Maybe this is the world trying to teach me you are a person. People forget that."

'I had no hard feelings, but it was interesting to hear,' says Landis. 'They don't know you, you're just the subject of whatever debate is going on at the time. The only guy it doesn't seem to affect is Donald Trump. He seems to be able to embrace it or just doesn't care, but fuck knows what's going on with that guy's head. But everyone else, at least in some way, it gets to you and it changes you. Whether you are human or not is irrelevant to people. But what it does to the people on my side of this, it's hard to find someone to relate to it, so you don't bother to even talk to anyone about it, because how could they possibly understand? It's not them in the situation, so they think what's the big deal? Ignore these people, why worry about it?

'And it's weird, too, as it's almost like being famous is a thing onto itself. Half the people you read about and that everyone pays attention to online don't really have anything extraordinary going on. They just happen to be the person that everyone is watching for no reason. Those people, I don't know what happens to them when the lights go out and everyone moves onto the next person. I don't know what they do as their only claim to fame is fame.'

That's McGregor without fighting.

A reality star to build up and smash down.

It's a dangerous game.

* * *

BACK IN 2016, THE *NEW YORK POST* RAN AN ARTICLE
entitled 'Dying for fame'. It was about the 21 reality stars in the United
States that committed suicide over the previous decade. It affected
the entire width of the genre, from small programmes like *Storage
Wars* to ratings winners like *The Bachelor*. Even peripheral figures like
Russell Armstrong, the husband of one of the cast members on *Real
Housewives of Beverly Hills*, hanged himself in 2011 after his marital
problems became the subject of must-see television. Before taking his
life, he told one journalist that it 'was pretty overwhelming. It took our
manageable problems and made them worse.'

Eliza Orlins, who starred in two seasons of *Survivor*, the reality show
where contestants become castaways on an island in Fiji, admitted that
people 'aren't screened by the shows as well as they should be', while
Jesse Csincsak, the fourth-season winner of *The Bachelorette*, added, 'A
lot of people have trouble dealing with the aftermath. I think people
don't realise the repercussions when they sign up … Over the course
of eight episodes, 50 million people saw them. Everywhere they go –
walking down the streets, on Facebook – all these people are judging
them. They didn't sign up to be portrayed as the bully or the slut or the
drunk or whatever, but they were, because that creates ratings equal
dollars.'

In a sense, sport ought to be different, as it's not staged or scripted.
But in terms of what its own famous faces go through, it has become
the same as so many other areas: those that achieve are added to the

long list of celebrities we are obsessed with. I mention to Landis that right before we spoke, skier Mikaela Shiffrin was being interviewed on CNN after a brilliant season on the slopes. However, while the main chyron read, 'Ski Superstar Shiffrin breaking record', the sub-heading was more revealing. 'Shiffrin has over 800k followers on Instagram.' Any and all measured by popularity, or just recognisability.

'I don't know, man, that's pretty bleak,' replies Landis. 'I'd never advise anyone I cared about to try fame. For me, part of the problem was I won the Tour and a couple of days later, it was still the big story, and the positive test came out, and I couldn't go and race, obviously. So I didn't have anything to do except read the news, and it becomes an obsession, you get fixated on it. I knew better than to read it, but I couldn't help it. I don't know if that's normal, like do these people now sit there and read all the comments on their Instagram or whatever? Is that what keeps them going? Depending on your personality, I guess, it takes over and I kept on trying to fight it, and that makes it worse, and it made me just want to drink, because I knew I was powerless to do anything about it.

'Drink was a way to numb, to switch off. I had a hip replacement within a couple of weeks, so they prescribed all this oxycontin and all these narcotics for me. I'd just drink alcohol and take some of those and just check out. A nice, warm, and happy feeling. This is a terrible thing to say, but that kind of kept me alive. I don't think I could have handled that otherwise. Maybe that's the wrong message to send, but alcohol and drugs helped me. There was nothing else I could do. I went to some psychologists and I'd tell the story, and they'd go, "Holy shit." So I cannot imagine at Conor's level. And his is a brutal sport. Those are different human beings to me, I don't know how they do what they do. And then this is his life when he's done with fighting in a cage? That's tough, man. I hope it doesn't end badly. Like, some people talk about him and cocaine. I did cocaine a couple of times and can see how you get hooked badly. I couldn't afford it, so that was my way out.'

If the rumours and allegations around that side of McGregor's life are true, it makes for a fascinating look in from the outside. Having created this pressure to play the character, thus widening the gulf between who he is and what we see, perhaps it's how he bridges that gap. If there is any truth in these allegations, he wouldn't be the first, and won't be the last, to let chemicals set his mind free as it cannot work out a way to close the chasm.

The problem is, he isn't alone in this.

'That's it, it's not just the celebrity,' says Landis. 'For those around me, they went through similar trauma because of me. The worst part was despair on their part as they were looking on and there was nothing they could do. They're helpless, you are helpless. Others didn't care and had made up their mind and were judging. But people that cared said, "Floyd, whatever we can do, we'll do." But they didn't know what to do. I think some of these things just take time; it doesn't matter what your mental fortitude is. And some people are just lucky. I watch some, though, have their meltdowns, and you never know what's going on behind the scenes, but it's not uncommon. It's sad, but there's no one to go to. There are no decent support groups as it's such a tiny amount of people that are on that level and that have to endure it. Usually, what helps is talking things through with someone who understands, but you just can't fucking find anybody.'

Looking back, that fame, just like the Tour de France, seems more like a film to him.

He knows it happened, but he can't remember feeling anything. That was just the psychological safety, a coping mechanism. 'Back then, even at my level, I didn't like the idea that people might be looking at me, or maybe it was all in my head. But I'm fairly sensitive about what people think about me. I try to get over that, but I do care, and at the end of the day, in order to be a decent human being, you need to care, as you want people to care what you think. I think at some point I became detached from it.'

It brings us back to McGregor, with those around him saying he has the same obsession with those who talk about him. It battles with the other part of him. One person close to him says he often craves the quiet life, although that's a view of himself he cannot project, for his followers don't like the idea. But away from them, a domestic life brings out the best.

Silence. Calm. Routine.

'It's not a way to live that brings any real happiness,' concludes Landis. 'You are constantly trying to create an image, and no one that is famous has an image that really reflects who they are. They have to try and alter it in some way, as it won't get you to where you think you want to go. You have to act when you are in public, and it becomes a full-time job, to the point it alters who you are. Most healthy people wouldn't want it if they understood what it really felt like. I feel sorry [for] those who have it.

'Look what you get from it, and then look at what you pay for it.'

As great as it may seem, and as great as he pretends it is, if this is the secret, then McGregor can keep it. But speaking with Landis brings back that image from the documentary of McGregor being chased down by the mob and wanting out.

It's exactly why they say no man is a hero to his valet.

CHAPTER 11

THIS IS A WHITE MAN'S WORLD

IN THE RUN-UP TO THE MCGREGOR FIGHT, POLITICS squeeze their way onto the odd TV set lining walls in hotels, casinos and bars. Usually, when not prime-time for some sports betting.

On such occasions the on-going story has been around the appointment of judge Brett Kavanaugh to the United States Supreme Court, despite allegations of sexual impropriety dating back to his adolescence. It's fascinating to step off the stage and play no part, instead taking a front-row seat and watching the reactions of others.

Early one morning, as his accuser Christine Blasey Ford started her testimony to the Senate hearing committee, she said that she was terrified and, as she continued and recounted the alleged sexual assault that took place back in high school, those watching on here had long made up their minds based on political allegiances rather than what was before them. One guy hammered down his glass with an attention-grabbing clank as she talked, but soon his mood hit a major upswing as Kavanaugh was before the mic and the nation.

The judge answered one question with, 'I like beer, do you like beer senator, what do you like to drink?' He responded to another query with, 'You're asking about, yeah, blackouts. I don't know, have you …? Yeah, I'm curious if you have?' He suggested that a reference to the well-known devil's triangle was about a drinking game when it's accepted as a threesome with two men and one woman. He said, in a supposed position where being apolitical is a cornerstone, that there's a left-wing conspiracy against him.

'You tell 'em,' came a roar. For the guys watching in Vegas liked beer and they had blackouts and they despised communism.

Kavanaugh talked their talk.

Kavanaugh walked their walk.

Whatever happened to holding people in higher positions to higher accountability?

This virus spreads though.

To law makers. To moral leaders. To standard bearers. To societal influencers.

The more you consider the trend, the more it becomes clear that McGregor, like so many others infected with entitlement via fame and bank balances, is thriving in a world that's in grave decline. He may not even believe many of them himself, but he openly hands out those words of hate based on identity, and makes money off those who do believe. Though the McGregor-Mayweather fight was clearly a myth of a contest, with the result all but determined beforehand, the build-up did at least give us a glimpse into how modern sport and entertainment can thrive in the current political climate.

It quickly became clear that the event fitted in so well with a

Trumpian moment in history, a sporting reflection of a broader shift. There we had the white guy who could trash talk better than the African-American and it lined up so well with the identity politics of the US president. More than that, it fitted in so perfectly with the notion that whites, and white men in particular, had been victimised and it was time to take a stand. Suddenly there was this embrace of McGregor, the person not afraid to shout it out. He had been masterful in that, walking a fine line between what could get him in trouble even in this new order, while always hinting. Many saw him through this as a very positive influence and a bearer of this white male potency.

The greater worry as attention span runs dry is what happens next?

A sign of these changing times is that he was once so controversial but has been normalised within a few short years. That's a warning to other areas of society that are far more important and influential than he ever can or will be.

Chaos can quickly be accepted.

Chaos can quickly be regularised.

* * *

THE SAYING GOES THAT ENTITLEMENT AND PRIVILEGE corrupt equally.

Right now both traits are rampant, owing largely to power, fame and fortune.

If we get both those traits in politics and entertainment, then we get them in sport too. McGregor has become a glorious example of that. However, he's far from alone.

Sports used to provide us with heroes and crusaders, with people we could look up to for the right reasons and imagine being like for good reasons.

For the most part, gone are those times. This area like others has had a wave crash over it, wiping out what stood before.

It's the same day as McGregor's open workout, where many down drinks and shout out boozed-up anger about 'faggots' as he prances around close to naked on stage. However, another story breaks that should be the biggest tale in town and, by a distance, the biggest sporting news taking place anywhere on the planet. A rape allegation has been made against Cristiano Ronaldo, so I grab a taxi to take in a story that could be talked about for months, if not for generations. As the taxi snakes its way across the city to the suburbs, the saying that 'What happens in Vegas stays in Vegas' comes to mind. Finally finding the lawyer's office where the accuser's legal team is holding a press conference, the handful of journalists that have showed make it feel distinctly small time.

Once more, in the realm of celebrity, it's not what you're alleged to have done, but who you are that counts.

Cristiano Ronaldo was at the hotel back in 2009 with the accuser as CCTV proves, and leaked emails from him allege that he told his lawyers he had even apologised to the woman, stating, 'Sorry, I'm usually a gentleman.' That night, she went and had a rape kit assembled which showed violent sex had taken place. Then there was the pay-off and non-disclosure agreement, a part of the law that affords the wealthy a potential pass and a way above the consequences. None of that matters, though. One Latin correspondent asks a question that makes the accused out as the victim. This is 2018 after all.

Elsewhere, it's no different. Go on social media and that's a line many take. Ronaldo couldn't have done this purely on the basis he is a good footballer and plays for a team people like. In fact, those that come out most harshly against him do so only for that same reason. They don't like his club, therefore an alleged rape is a sporting chance to score points. This is what we've been reduced to. This is what we have fostered. It all sounds so similar to the law makers up on the hill in Washington across recent days. (Ronaldo denied the allegations and in July 2019 prosecutors said that he would not face criminal charges over the allegations.)

It's accepted, though, because of our value system of putting a person above their actions, our entertainment above others' pain. This is what McGregor now inhabits as, twenty minutes back across town and he's finished up standing in front of a chanting crowd.

'Fuck the Jameson brothers.'

Out of the frying pan and into this fire.

The Irish fans spend the evening up and down the strip with tricolours and plastic cups, regurgitating what he's said about his opponent. I ask one guy from Dublin why he thinks it's okay for McGregor to slag Khabib Nurmagomedov based on him being a Muslim who doesn't drink. 'Cause he's fucking loaded. You'll never make that money.'

Then comes the predictable rant about jealously, bitterness, and begrudgery.

These are the sheep.

In the zone of sports writing, you become privy to a chapter's worth of troubling stories. Some heroes you really shouldn't meet. Take this as a starter from a few years back. A well known player for a country at the 2018 World Cup that failed in the groups was in a busy living room at a house party, when he demanded one of the female guests perform oral sex on him there in front of some teammates. When she refused, he spat in her face.

And on it goes. Give an inch. Take someone's dignity.

It's not just about women, but that is one form where life on a pedestal can be best seen at its worst. In 2014, Australian journalist Anna Krien documented the cult of power and sex that exists in sport in her award-winning book *Night Games*. There were many instances, such as 'pranks' involving swapping partners in the dark, of gangbangs being a rite of passage, of it being overlooked with one club actually warning players 'to make sure she leaves happy and then she won't complain'. Krien surmised it thus: 'Treating women like shit shades into a culture of abuse, which in turn can shade into rape.' And this at a time when we often mistakenly look to celebrity for guidance.

Yet we know all this and have done for some time, and despite all that, there's still little stigma in sport or in society around it, no matter how bad it gets. We can pretend there is, but if it was really seen that badly, it wouldn't be happening on an industrial scale.

We have got our value systems beyond muddled. There are a startling number of men who are happy to hide behind boys-will-be-boys and she-was-asking-for-it undertones. Locker room talk, as Trump calls it.

If you want to delve into the psychology of it in terms of sportsmen and sex, there's a case to be made around their view of a success involving someone else failing. There's a case to be made about praise for their aggressive and dominant on-field behaviour and them exhibiting that same behaviour off it. There's a case to be made that it's not just sportsmen but men in general, with their belief in their right to do as they want both heightened and excused by celebrity status.

How much tolerance is needed, and how much understand-ing is acceptable? Some sensible points have been made, with calls for sporting associations to address their male athletes, but even wise words take us back to that troublesome confusion. For instance, should adults actually have to be taught the most basic morality because they are good at sport? Must we try and reconcile the most simple notion of care and respect with a need to educate on common decency?

So where does a journey that sees a person end up here begin?

Looking down on people around you?

Thinking you can get your way around the little things?

If so, it bodes ill for this people's champion.

* * *

HERE IN VEGAS, CONOR MCGREGOR MAY NOT HAVE

ended up as badly as those cases, but he has ticked so many boxes that you get the feeling it's out of control and won't end well. The train going too fast always comes to a corner and hurtles off the tracks, and this cannot last forever.

He oozes a lunatic streak that is only briefly brought back to some semblance of normality when a fight is announced. It steals back his focus for a couple of months while giving him further leeway once he's done with it.

Short-term salvation. Medium-term destruction.

At all other times, he overcompensates, but for what? And this is an extreme case which is some going considering the many others that have pockmarked combat sports in particular. He really is a projection of those he grew up around and where he grew up, with the uglier elements tied up tight in that. All that front has to be to cover up something and someone deeply insecure. It's hard to be confident given where he comes from. It's as if he doesn't belong here and he knows it.

'Fuck the Jameson Brothers,' rings out again.

Who is he to be on a stage in Vegas, not just winning in his sport but winning in business and winning in Sin City by sinning most? Thus he resorts to being the icon in the age of exposure, hiding behind all publicity, whether it's good or bad. If people are talking about this, then at least they aren't probing around what he fears most. His weakness.

Back at the start he was motivated by the right reasons. Now, even with this fight speeding over the horizon, it can be hard to think this is nothing but a business. It's not about being the best he can but proving to everyone he's this wild gangster. As if it's all to remind that he's still that guy when really, he's very far from reality doing this stuff and getting away with it.

Is there a way out?

He isn't helping himself.

Those around him don't help.

The time and place certainly doesn't help.

His fans want him like this. They admire what isn't admirable.

So this is his town. A place that plays on the doubts and weaknesses of many. A place with no soul. A place where cash can buy you anything. A place where cash is an excuse for everything. There's only so much of it you can take, and it's best to escape it all.

A long day involving various projections of a similar message is exhausting. From the Senate hearing to McGregor, to his fans, to the Cristiano Ronaldo press conference.

Back in the sanctuary of my hotel room, I turn on the TV and on comes an ad for the R&B strip club. It involves some miserable-looking women dancing in what looks like no more than a bare and dank garage. Beside them, a rapper with gold on each and every finger shouts into a microphone. 'Money, money, money, money, money, money ...'

CHAPTER 12

IMPROPER 12

IN 2017, ESPN JOURNALIST WRIGHT THOMPSON shacked up in Dublin and went on out into areas like the ones I pass through on this February day.

Across Crumlin and Drimnagh, his aim was to try to get a sense of what made Conor McGregor tick so well and, at times, what brought about the loud, mistimed thud of a tock we are getting so sadly used to. There was excellent access given the need to sell the Floyd Mayweather fight to the United States' pay-per-view market, and also given the weight and influence his publication carries within that massive market.

There was incredible insight too, though, as we've come to expect from the Mississippi native. So, this morning on a bus through a part of the city that Thompson also traversed, I pull up his article. It's more revealing now than even at the time, which says a lot.

On the fighter's delicate nature, hidden in the hope of being lost and forgotten, he wrote: 'McGregor, for all his bravado, can be fragile. Norman Mailer wrote about approaching Ali's psyche like you'd approach a squirrel. That's true for Conor too.'

On a Houdini-style act that sees the fighter confused and wondering how exactly he pulled off his own escape, he mused: 'There's just something in the way Conor is wired. That's one of the reasons [John] Kavanagh didn't bring in coaches with more boxing experience. Too much stuff, by someone who didn't approach Conor's psyche like a squirrel, would be a disaster. McGregor, at his core, is an act of imagination. Tell the truth about someone, he said once, and they crumble. His truth is that he's an apprentice plumber from Crumlin trying to shake off the inevitability of those facts. He's escaped so many traps that he now instinctively seeks them out.'

On the fighter's split and contrasting personality, he wrote: 'He's obsessed with his social media accounts. There's a line between the online image he has cultivated and his actual home life with his family. Beloved Irish boxer Michael Conlan, who knows McGregor, calls the public and private man "like chalk and cheese – complete opposites". Drawing such a line, creating a character to sell, always carries the same risk: losing control of your creation and actually becoming the preening egomaniac you once only pretended to be. He's risen to a level known by only a select few, where the air is thin and the margins are slim. If you can catch a glimpse of him when he doesn't know you're looking, he seems human-sized and vulnerable. Conor's bravado suggests a scared kid still in there somewhere, trying to keep many things at bay, most vitally his own fear that his journey could be a circle.'

On what scares the fighter most, he proclaimed: 'Even as someone like McGregor is rising, his fall feels close enough to touch. Nearly all famous fighters end up back where they started, busted, a punch-drunk eulogy to their inability to escape whatever first drove them to fight. McGregor brags he's gonna eat lobster for the rest of his life while his critics and opponents will eat their words. Maybe that's true. When you meet him, and see the pride in his eyes when he talks of giving his new-born son a different kind of life, you want it to be true. He's making lots of money, and spending lots of money, and the thing his family and friends fear most isn't the next opponent but the moment when he no longer has an opponent.'

Yet it was none of that which nearly broke the internet in Ireland. Such a level of insight and dissection was too much for many who just wanted to roar on a lump of muscle who waved around wads of cash, while not having to consider and deal with the principle that what goes up must also come down. So, instead, they focused on a line of Thompson's that had actually been changed by an editor and didn't read as it had been intended initially.

'It's a clannish, parochial place,' it said of Dublin, and specifically these boroughs. 'Crossing the wrong street has traditionally been reason enough for an ass-whipping. Men have had to drop dates off at bus stops instead of walking them all the way home.' Over the top, sure, but when that article was published and some took to their keyboards to have a pot-shot at the micro as it allowed for escapism and deflection from the uncomfortable and truth-telling macro, how many of them had a clue what was, and is, going on?

To understand this part of McGregor's being, you have to understand his surrounds. Such has been his home patch, it was all around him. Such has been his sport, it has stayed all around him. Such is his life, it will likely remain all around him for as long as he makes it.

* * *

THERE'S AN UNDERGROUND IN DUBLIN YOU WON'T hear about openly in bars or boxing clubs. Instead, the *omertá* means that whispers are hidden away.

We tend not to know what's being discussed until after it's acted upon. Indeed, if sport is a microcosm of life, then the fight game is so often a microcosm of this gang life.

Before mixed martial arts and McGregor came along, that fight game in the Irish capital was boxing. And those on the wrong side of the law regularly took a keen interest: crime boss Gerry Hutch was a major player in the sweet science when his later rival Daniel Kinahan was only a kid. But years on, it became Kinahan's passion also, as they went to war.

Kinahan and his cartel are not only the major player in the Irish cocaine market, but across Europe. To get a sense of scale here, in 2010, a series of raids called Operation Shovel discovered over €150 million worth of Kinahan-connected properties in Ireland and Spain, Belgium and Dubai, South Africa, Brazil and Cyprus. It means that from a sporting perspective, when you want to dip a toe into what he's done within boxing, there's a massive evasion from others within the game. Fighters. Promoters. Trainers.

No matter whom I try and approach, there's worry.

Fear of biting the hand that feeds you? Or just plain fear?

For the most part, calls end up going dead, text offers are refused, WhatsApps have their tick go blue but are ignored, while voicemails don't produce any valuable response.

One person agreed to talk, only under the condition of not just anonymity but an actual encrypted line. 'It says much about boxing in Ireland that just to chat about an aspect of a sport, it has to be like this,' they say. Another making a living from it notes that if they were approached by the Kinahans and 'told to walk away from all I have in boxing, I'd do it instantly'. They add, 'You'd be better off staying away from it, too.'

That's not a choice, though, when looking at McGregor. Some strings are knotted so tightly, they cannot be untangled.

So let's return to the beginning of this sorry mess.

Back before McGregor had his first UFC fight, former Irish middle-weight and world super-welterweight contender Matthew Macklin founded Macklin's Gym in Marbella, Spain. Due to legal issues with the MGM hotel, that name was later changed to Mack The Knife, or MTK. He initially saw this gym as a community asset, something to give back but, as it grew much bigger and spread to other locations, the downside was having Daniel Kinahan as the co-founder. The two were and are still close mates, but while the former was the face, that slowly changed over time as the latter grew more confident in terms of what he could add, and what the gym could do for him.

Boxing to Kinahan has been described by those close to the organised crime scene as what football was to Pablo Escobar in his pomp. Sources note that he's long had an obsession with the sport. It was also a void he could fill, for the pro game has always struggled in the Republic, to the point that only a handful of tickets were sold when Lennox Lewis came to town 1995, with the rest thrown out like confetti in order to give the fight-night optics less the feel of a disaster. Meanwhile, when Prince Naseem Hamed showed up in Dublin as champion, he had to engage in an open workout on Grafton Street to garner interest before he got near the canvas. In essence, it was a graveyard.

But Kinahan is not only a very good manager, he was also willing to put rare money in. Quickly, MTK grew and was a player in European boxing the same way Kinahan had taken over European cocaine. It was claustrophobic and ruthless, with little room for others.

For a while, Kinahan's importance in boxing boomed to the point where he was close to stepping out from the shadow of his father, Christy. Known as 'The Dapper Don' for obvious reasons, he'd led and expanded the family business for years. He served time in jail where he learnt French so, crime correspondents say, he could better communicate around transactions coming out of north Africa. In time, he passed on more authority to his son.

This move to boxing, though, was like something from *The Godfather III*, for very few make the move from being in organised crime to being a legitimate businessman. Granted, boxing is one of few sports that can make it happen without too many questions asked or too many eyebrows raised. By early 2016, Daniel Kinahan was on the verge of this very move, ready for a new and seemingly above-board life.

But for him, trying to separate his boxing ambitions from his cartel career had never been easy. In August 2014, a Hutch gunman attempting to assassinate him mistakenly shot former Irish super-welterweight champion Jamie Moore in the hip and leg in Marbella, leaving him lucky to be alive. It was a close call, and soon it would be closer. On 5 February 2016, at the weigh-in for the European title bout between McGregor's friend Jamie Kavanagh and Antonio João Bento in the Regency Hotel, Hutch gunmen infiltrated proceedings – some dressed as Garda special unit, another as a woman. They opened fire in a crowded room, and McGregor's former neighbour David Byrne was killed. The intended target, Kinahan, had left early and, while he survived, his dreams of making it away from the drug game died.

Such is the threat to his life today that it has recently been reported he's left his Spanish surrounds and is holed up in Dubai, surrounded by ex-Russian special forces bodyguards.

Suddenly, MTK's links to organised crime became clear, even to those who didn't know the underworld. This was it crawling to the surface, and outrage abounded. As a person close to it previously told me, 'Hutch is a strategist, and he destroyed Kinahan's rise as a boxing manager in that moment when he picked the weigh-in for that attack.'

It created havoc thereafter. The Boxing Union of Ireland (BUI) became wary of MTK fighters, with its president at the time, Mel Christle, stating, 'The reality is that the presence of an MTK fighter on a bill at present, in the view of the Boxing Union, would put at risk the safety of patrons and other persons involved in the boxing event. It's as simple as that.' By the start of 2018, MTK had the plug pulled on shows. At one stage, the Garda wouldn't commit to providing security but when that was eventually thrashed out, and with five fighters on the card for a night in CityWest Hotel here in Dublin, the return was on. The media reported six Garda armed units were in waiting, but the hotel had second thoughts and got out.

But there's a key question here: while the BUI were worried, and that shooting ought to have ended Kinahan's fight-game ambitions, did it do so?

It's a logical query based on what we know rather than a wild and easy accusation. That's because in October 2017, MTK was taken over by Sandra Vaughan, who has an entertaining history as well.

A former hairdresser, by 2008 she had amassed a fortune and paid £10m in order to buy out the Fake Bake tanning and beauty business that would get endorsements from the likes of Madonna. She has never been implicated in wrongdoing, but associations still drew plenty of unwanted attention, to the point where both her home and company were raided by the Scottish Crime and Drug Enforcement Agency in August 2010. Such associations included her previous partner, Kevin Kelly, whom she met after he was jailed for six years in 1995 for dealing ecstasy and cannabis, although they're reported to have split in 2005. He went on to front a Marbella-based business with Daniel Kinahan. In 2012, he was rescued by Spanish police, having been kidnapped, tied to a bed, tortured, and beaten by what the Spanish government said was 'the Irish mafia'.

Come 2013, Fake Bake UK was liquidated and Vaughan had married Danny Vaughan, a trainer at MTK Global. Danny, as an aside, is a convicted benefit fraudster and did ten months in jail for for his part in a £100,000 scam. So how many degrees of separation from Kinahan to MTK does that sound like?

On top of that look at the comments from some of those in their stable. On social media the hugely promising super-lightweight Jack Catterall boasted he is still 'advised by' Kinahan. Meanwhile, in a since-deleted tweet, another MTK fighter Stephen Simmons said 'all chats' must go through MTK, Matthew Macklin, who has remained on the board in an advisory capacity, and Kinahan too.

As much as things change, they seem the same. It cannot be confirmed, but with some suggesting Kinahan still rests somewhere in the background of a company in which he played such a key part, one source hints the ultimate dream is one of the superfights in the United States. In essence, a McGregor-style extravaganza involving tens of millions. Tyson Fury, who is on the MTK books, seems the obvious option, but had the Regency Hotel not happened, timing meant it could've been McGregor.

That would have been quite a thing, considering where he and the cartel emerged from along these Crumlin streets.

* * *

'YOU'LL BE SUED IF YOU GO NEAR THIS PART OF IT,' says one person close to him about the idea of bringing up a key element of McGregor's life.

'The truth isn't libel,' I remind them.

It's little wonder they try to micro-manage this, though, as the most constructive and destructive part of him is the act that he doesn't care that much. Like Trump in a sense, McGregor appears to believe that the only thing worse than being talked about is not being talked about. It also plays into the creation that people line up to buy.

It means he's never been shy about who he's hung around with. In part, you can be sure that adds to the image of the ghetto gangster. Just like rappers sell their false anger and rage to white, teenage boys who go to the shopping mall with their parents' credit card, so much of the McGregor myth is targeting white men in their twenties who still live at home. It's a world they would never survive in, but this gets them close enough to touch it.

Straight out of Crumlin.

Growing up, McGregor will have known plenty of those that would take a different and dangerous path to wealth. It means he still knows them. That's just life. In one sense, there's a loyalty and nobility in it, much like the dog sleeping beside the passed-out tramp. The problem is, though, that the tramp tends to only destroy himself and not others.

So what's the balance here? You decide.

You don't choose where you are from and, despite the trite saying, you don't choose your friends. It means that guilt should not be via association. This is who he is and, besides, the fighter is always drawn to the gangster and the gangster to the fighter. They are, after all, attracted as archetypes. So, perhaps, what protrudes is a disappointment rather than blame around who McGregor rolls with. Having once had the chance to show possibilities to those who live around his neighbourhood here, he now indulges those who destroy that very neighbourhood.

Could he have stepped away from that world and these people?

Should he have stepped away from that world and these people?

Either way, he didn't. To look at McGregor's links to all of this, you almost need a whiteboard. And connecting his name to those in the cartel, you quickly spin a web.

As the *Irish Independent* pointed out in 2016, 'A group of a dozen young thugs closely associated with members of the Kinahan Cartel have been described as "the next generation" of lieutenants in the capital. The group of 12 young men and teenagers from the south Dublin area are described as being "extremely loyal" to cartel member Liam Byrne ... Sources have revealed how a number of the young men were flown to Las Vegas for a Conor McGregor fight last year, with tens of thousands believed to have been spent on the group trip.' Indeed, in the lead-up to the Nurmagomedov loss, a joint operation between US customs and the Garda saw 53 people prevented from boarding flights to Vegas. Some had criminal convictions already, others were excluded because of suspicion around such Kinahan cartel links.

A few years ago, when a turf war began between elements in Drimnagh and those in Crumlin, the latter prevailed. Making up that group were the likes of Liam Byrne and a batch of relatives. That's seen by the authorities across Europe as a major strength of theirs, as not only are the police trying to break into a criminal gang but also a family. At the bottom end is a new and brash generation that flaunt whatever they have to a degree that experts in this area worry for them in the medium-term at best. Reared on the cartel, they know nothing else, and it's these who McGregor is so often seen with and seen indulging. For instance, when he was photographed standing on the bonnet of that Rolls-Royce in Liverpool, the person with him was Lee Byrne – Liam's son.

But the main links are via the Murray brothers, with whom he travels all the time. They are career drug dealers with a serious rap sheet. Jonathan has 48 criminal convictions – including four for drug dealing. Andrew Murray is listed as having eighteen priors, including drug possession with intent for sale or supply, theft, and forgery. There's also the 2012 case of an assault on Joey O'Brien, a protected state witness who was giving evidence in a gangland murder trial. Spotted one night in a Chinese takeaway on Dame Street in the Irish capital, Jonathan was involved in punching him to the ground, calling him a rat, and literally dancing on his head. O'Brien woke up the next morning in hospital with a broken jaw, smashed teeth, a fractured eye socket, a concussion, and no memory of the incident. Then just 22, Murray got eighteen months in prison.

Both of the Murrays' timelines on social media are littered with pictures of them and McGregor, dating as far back as 2014. They're regularly seen on McGregor's yacht, and they were with him in December 2017 when he appeared with R&B star Rita Ora at the British Fashion Awards. Ora captioned a social media photograph with him 'date night' to much backlash given his relationship status, and McGregor was later that night photographed with a group of strippers. It's clear he's more comfortable with them than the likes of Ora, for you can take the boy out of Crumlin, but not Crumlin out of the boy.

The gangland links have led to increasingly wild rumours about the nature of McGregor's financial affairs, but there has been no evidence to ever support them. Simply think back to November 2017 and the incident in the Black Forge, just up the road where McGregor was alleged to have punched the father of the notorious Graham 'The Wig' Whelan in a bar fight.

High up in the cartel's Birmingham operation, Whelan is a head-down guy who hangs in the background, doesn't drive fancy cars or flaunt his money, and is believed to be hugely dangerous. It was his sister who first posted on social media about the row in the pub, but then it got out of control. Next, there was talk of McGregor's life being on the line, of grovelling to Daniel Kinahan, and of a six-figure pay-off to make it go away. Floyd Mayweather had a pop, to which McGregor replied, 'I am the cartel.' Kinahan himself responded to Mayweather's tweet with, 'Now now should not believe all you read in the paper, must be looking for a rematch against [McGregor]'.

Of course, none of it was true, and as it went viral and hit the news from Australia to the States, a small part of Dublin found it hugely funny. It was all part of Planet McGregor. And it was all part of Planet Cartel. It was a sign, too, of modern celebrity status that enveloped both and envelopes all.

But it also shows that Wright Thompson, for all the abuse he got, wasn't that wrong. What few knew is that shortly after the publication of his article, members of McGregor's team got in touch and asked that it be removed. They said McGregor's parents were very worried that his words could be deemed worthy of reprisal.

As Thompson put it best in his article: 'Crumlin to Crumlin, with a fairytale in between.'

That applies to them all, not just McGregor.

After everything, Thompson was too close to the bone.

CHAPTER 13

I'LL BE THERE IN A MINUTE

THERE'S ANGER IN THE AIR.

At least that's what those going through the security screening for this Las Vegas press conference are telling one another. Two days to go. The wait nearly over. But the wait for what?

If anything, there's frustration rather than anger, and mainly due to the long, loping queues, the sort you would find at an airport. It's not helped by the McGregor fans, who are filling bins with half-full cans they've been trying to chug having been told there's no way they're getting them inside.

'It'll be worth the wait.'

So those who eventually make it past the security screening tell each other. This they believe a little more as they head on into the auditorium.

This is where it truly begins. Except there's a problem.

It's here Dana White stands at a podium centre-stage, and rather than promote the bubbling fury that makes this a pay-per-view goldmine, he is soothing the frustration, while beside him Khabib Nurmagomedov sits all alone. There's that telltale focus on the Russian's square face that should be an important insight for those paying close attention. Few are looking for such hints, though, for they were supposed to be here for some trash-talking and hopefully an impromptu punch-up.

So this is where it truly begins? Well, you need two to tango.

'Conor's not here yet,' says White, as if we cannot see that for ourselves. There's a cheer because his name has been spoken. 'Khabib said he's not going to wait.' There's a boo because *his* name has been spoken.

It's like a Christmas pantomime, only Conor isn't and won't be behind Khabib, as he's late. Again.

One more mind game? Or, given his opponent and the failure of such mind games thus far, some real mental weakness?

From Khabib, there is no weakness.

He's icy and brutal, like one of those automatons from his country portrayed in American cinema during the Cold War. Back then, such propaganda gave his side no emotion for audiences to cling onto, allowing a clear distinction around the bad guy. But looking at him, there's so much to admire about it. In an era of endless sports debate and pseudo-psychology, how does a person stay so cool when the heat keeps on being turned up to boiling point? It's amazing to behold. A special skill you cannot be taught.

He's asked about what it's like to be up there by himself. 'I don't wait for nobody,' he replies. 'This is 3pm, everyone is here. I said 3pm I begin. If you guys have a question, that's cool.' Two days out from a fight, such is the inability of the modern psyche to sit still, the next question is about what happens after this. 'Honestly, I don't know, I'm not underestimating this guy. I'm preparing, my weight is good. After, we will see.'

Bored, the crowd belt out that borrowed Irish soccer chant they've long made their own. 'Olé, Olé, Olé.' It's like a Mexican wave at a football match, when you can tell the action is lacking as fans resort to self-amusement. Khabib sounds like a normal athlete, but the crowd didn't come here for such down-to-earth conversation.

'Listen, man, I'm excited,' White interjects, as if he's Vince McMahon trying not to lose the precious audience on WWE Raw. He cuts through the disinterested noise. 'I can't wait for the weigh-ins and the fight. Conor's in a car, he'll be here in a few minutes.'

He's making excuses for his man.

Lately he's always been making excuses for his man.

It's a real sign of his man but also of his organisation and where it finds itself.

This is never good in any sport, for it suggests that someone has become bigger than the business. It's a road to nowhere, as no one benefits from such a scenario. The likes of Mo Farah could miss doping tests and blame it on not hearing a doorbell, and the IAAF wouldn't say a bad word because he brought in the crowds. Serena Williams is similar in that it was simply accepted when she locked herself into a panic room when a tester called at her door and, on a follow-up occasion, she had a direct line to the head of women's tennis to complain about such a violation of her time and space. Meanwhile, Tiger Woods was a mess and had it brushed under the carpet, to the point that it ended up crippling him.

McGregor can do no wrong in the same way. White is proof of it. Hearing and seeing that, Nurmagomedov quietly seethes. Biding his time. Soon. It's like every little instance and incident is jotted down and tucked away at the very forefront of his cranium for the time when it can be used best and most violently.

'If you talk about him going inside my head, you're going to see Saturday, you're going to see this,' he continues. 'I don't think about him. I have a schedule. I have to worry about myself.

'Why do I have to think about him? If somebody is late, that's not my problem ... My job is to control my emotion, to stay relaxed, keep going and maul this guy. It's most important to stay relaxed when you go to the cage. This is what matters.'

The crowd are restless again and this time interject with 'sheet the bus'. It's a reference to McGregor's line at the previous press conference, regarding his reaction to the attack in New York. The attempt at a Russian accent is embarrassing. The content more so.

But that night in the Big Apple was more to these people's liking, only there were no fans allowed. It made McGregor look like a clown away from the circus, like a bad sitcom without the canned laughter to cover its flaws. He just seemed nasty, almost panicking as he went beyond lines he'd stayed away from in the past. That wasn't strength. It was weakness.

'This is called prize fighting, but thankfully, I'm such a crafty individual with my other entities and my game as a whole, I don't have to fight for money no more,' he shouted in the silence of the arena over on the east coast a few weeks ago.

At times, he simply wound himself up because he couldn't get to Khabib. 'The bang of shite of you, mate, the bang of shite of you kid. I don't have to fight for money no more. I've made so much with my properties ... You're going to be wrestling my knuckle out of my orbital bone you shitebox. You smelly shitebag ... Fake, lying rat. There's a gorilla on my chest, I wear it proud. You're a lying rat ... When money got pumped into you by that scumbag that's down in a little eight-by-ten cell, you thought you were a Don. Now look at you. State of you. You haven't got a washer. I'm set for life, and this beautiful fine bottle of Irish whiskey is going to dominate the market. I'm coming to take over the whiskey business. This is a true beast I have in my possession.'

When none of that worked, McGregor got personal. He brought up Chechen dictator Ramzan Kadyrov and labelled the champion's father a coward for associating with him — as if you could ever say no to such a request, which was all that happened. 'Kadyrov is a crazy man, don't get me wrong. But, Khabib's father, lick-ass O'Hoolihan, posts a picture of Kadyrov at his mosque and the caption is, "Together we are stronger."'

Still unfazed, Khabib smirked as McGregor started drinking his whiskey in the latest marketing effort, and, when hearing it was his opponent's birthday, poured the devout Muslim a glass and tried to shove it in front of him. 'It's shite-on-the-bus's birthday. Here's a gargle for you, Dana. Happy birthday, shite on the bus.'

'I don't drink,' shrugged Khabib, refusing to be part of one more desperate ad.

'Why don't you drink?' fumed McGregor.

'I never drink.'

'I'd say you're some fun at parties, you mad, backwards cunt. You're dead when I get my hands on you. Me and the Irish animal Dana will suck down this bad boy.'

A trip to a chipper after the clubs in Dublin and you'd hear better, but the fans have paid to cross the globe to hear him say it to Khabib one more time. They've been counting down the days, the hours, the minutes.

But now, only Khabib is here and he's calm.

'He can say whatever he wants,' he goes on in relation to some jumped-up question around McGregor being safe in Russia in the future. 'Nobody cares about him. When we go to the cage, we will see who's going to talk ... This is weight day, I'm not waiting for thirty or forty minutes.' He taps his watch and looks at his team. Time is ticking on what is a mere distraction, as he has more important elements in his preparation to focus on. This is all about winning, not entertaining.

He says he will never shake McGregor's hand.

There are more boos at this.

He explains that it's personal now, after McGregor shoved that whiskey in his face the last time and then questioned his religious reasoning and manliness for not drinking it. 'This is more to defend my title. For me, it's personal ... I don't care about this. Most important is believing in myself.

'All the time, when he's tired, he gives up,' he adds. 'Before fights, he always talks about how he's ready for this. But when he fights with Diaz and Mayweather, when he's tired, he gives up all the time.'

And then he does something that throws the crowd off. He thanks the fans who have abused him, and they don't know how to react. They've been told he's the bad guy, and now this? There's muttering.

It's like watching refined composure. McGregor has got inside so many minds on the way up that so many opponents overcompensated to show it didn't bother them. Nurmagomedov puts up no such front.

Instead, there's just disinterest around this chatter before he gets to do what he wants to do. It's a mental toughness built on absolute belief in himself, in his ability, and what those two elements will mean to the result.

It's not even because McGregor isn't here, for when the Dubliner was at his loudest and most obnoxious, he looked on, past the noise, to the very core of an opponent that would be made to pay for that noise. Some will say that growing up in Dagestan helped in that regard, where crime rates are so high that M-1 Global, the Russian MMA promotion company, avoided doing events there and told their English-speaking commentators they couldn't guarantee they wouldn't be kidnapped. But José Aldo could attest to similar a background, and look what happened there. Yet even now, in advance, you could safely wager that

Khabib wouldn't crack in such a way.

It helps, too, that McGregor's act has become stale. The tune remains the same and when you've heard it over and over, turning up the sound doesn't make it original. You can't be controversial when everything is controversial as, by its definition, it becomes the norm. You can't surprise when your entire effort is expected. Instead, it's boring, predictable.

Ally that to Khabib. He's earned this and, unlike McGregor, there hasn't been the level of success and lifestyle to soften him. Maybe in time, but now he's at his most desperate, which means he's at his most dangerous.

His has been a lonely path, full of patience and introspection. He may have been a 16-0 fighter before joining the UFC for his first fight in 2012, but, while extremely dominant, he was also considered boring to watch. McGregor learned that winning wasn't enough: he needed a gimmick and an act, a character attached to the fighter. Instead, with Khabib, there was a lot more humility. When he won, comparisons were always made with Fedor Emelianenko, and whether Khabib could become the next great Russian combatant. He may have finally been getting some attention, but it was an insult in terms of ethnicity.

Frustratingly, it wasn't even his record that first got more casual attention. Khabib wore a T-shirt that said, 'If Sambo [a martial art and combat that originates from the Soviet Union] Was Easy It Would Be Called Jiu-Jitsu,' and it ended up all over the internet. Then came what those same people drawn to such meme-esque photos referred to as his 'white, furry hat' — a papakha. Suddenly, he was interesting, and even more so when he would celebrate by putting his hands together and praying.

The Eagle, as he started calling himself, had landed.

It was a subtle way to brand himself and a subtle way to attract a fan base. Until then, he had often found himself ignored. Contrast that to

McGregor and the instant attention that came his way straight away following his first UFC victory. Many people who follow the sport know where they were when they first saw him fight. Khabib? Not a chance. No one cared.

From that moment in 2013, McGregor's only speed bump was an ACL injury, and even that he overcame quickly. But Khabib's career has been riddled with road blocks. When he failed to cut the weight in Vegas when fighting Tony Ferguson, anger was such that people didn't want to see him near a title fight ever again. Plus there was his own litany of instances where his body broke down before the pressure.

A hard road created a hard man.

* * *

ZIYAVUDIN MAGOMEDOV IS A RUSSIAN OLIGARCH who made his money in finance and telecoms, but a fall out out with Vladimir Putin led to his arrest in March 2018. The official allegation was the embezzlement of $35m in funds intended for a World Cup stadium, but before that, he was a sponsor of several fighters — including Khabib.

This is an expensive game when you are getting action, but Khabib wasn't. Once, he was flown to Germany for a surgery nobody will talk about. It was bankrolled. As was the stipend he was paid to train away in America; as were the holidays home to Dagestan; as were the trips for both him and his growing team that number half a dozen to Bahrain, to Uzbekistan, to Kazakhstan, all to meet dignitaries as his name grew in that part of the planet.

It's an indictment of the UFC that someone of that talent wouldn't have made it this far without the backing of the sort of shady characters who allow even McGregor to cast aspirations. But the fight game has always been an example of a sporting arena where questionable money from up high pays those with nothing to beat each other for the entertainment of the judgmental middle. White is the latest to profit from that model, and while Khabib may have once felt like a beggar, it's all been for a moment like this.

For that reason he gets up and leaves the press conference. He's always struggled with the scales, and he's been through too much to give away any little advantage and to give McGregor any little satisfaction. As he goes, his manager Ali Abdelaziz walks away too, and the odd Irish tricolour rolled into a ball is flung at the entourage, with fans again chanting 'sheet the bus'.

On Khabib's manager, who has somehow been allowed to become a big player in the UFC, McGregor has never been wrong in his assessments, even if they were merely meant to rile his opponent. If Khabib is admirable, there's nothing to be in awe of with this guy.

He ruins the names of his fighters, like graffiti on an old stone wall.

There was the 2015 lawsuit filed against the World Series of Fighting that said Abdelaziz – at the time vice-president and matchmaker for WSOF – had a 'relationship to and control of an entity named Dominance, LLC'. The lawsuit alleged that Abdelaziz was in violation of the Nevada State Athletic Commission regulations. 'On several occasions, the sponsors for fighters managed by Dominance and those of WSOF were in conflict. When such conflicts arose, Mr. Abdeziz [sic] always favored the sponsors of Dominance over WSOF sponsors to the detriment of WSOF.'

The statement continued. 'Moreover, Aziz refused to make fights that were in the best interest of MMAWC and WSOF. Rather than choosing the fights that would generate the most fan interest and thus revenue for WSOF, Aziz set matches that favored his fighters and his pocket. Aziz also often refused to set fights for fighters that were not managed by him.'

There was his representation of Chechen and Dagestani fighters linked to Kadyrov through his Akhmat MMA gyms. From there, he forged another relationship with another authoritarian government known for massive human rights abuses, this time in Bahrain through one of the monarchy's princes, Sheikh Khalid bin Hamad Al-Khalifa.

But most striking was this.

On 11 September 2001, Abdelaziz was booked on a flight from Cairo to New York using a stolen passport with the name of a US citizen. The flight was cancelled because of the terror attacks that day, but he was later caught with five passports linked to Jamaat ul-Fuqra [a separatist group of mostly African-American Muslims based in Pakistan and the United States who have planned numerous acts of violence] and charged with various crimes including passport fraud, cheque fraud, and counterfeiting. In jail at age 25 near Denver, he was picked up as an informant by the NYPD. This part of his career is referenced by authors Matt Apuzzo and Adam Goldman, in the book *Enemies Within: Inside the NYPD's Secret Spying Unit and Bin Laden's Final Plot Against America.*

In it, they explain how Abdelaziz became an asset in the NYPD's efforts to break into the extremist group Muslims of America. In doing so, he became one of their best paid informants, earning hundreds of thousands for his efforts. Indeed, the NYPD also wanted to share their prized asset, known as Confidential Informant 184, with the FBI so they could continue their investigation beyond their jurisdiction.

It saw the bureau sponsor Abdelaziz, as his privileges and benefits continued to grow. In this instance, they gave him both money and a special green card as he travelled to and from Trinidad and Tobago and Venezuela among other destinations. There was just one problem. He was a liar. On 8 April 2008, the FBI told NYPD officials to bring Abdelaziz to the bureau's office, where agent Michael Templeton hooked him up to a polygraph.

As the book states:

The questions started simply.

'Are you now in New York City[?]'

'Are you currently employed?'

'Is today Friday?'

When Templeton asked Abdelaziz if he intended to be honest with the FBI about whether he'd told anybody that he was a government agent, Abdelaziz said yes. The machine said otherwise. Templeton seized on it. Polygraphers commonly use that question to spot double agents, people working as a spy for one agency but whose true loyalties lie with another. As he pressed Abdelaziz, the FBI agent began to believe that he had told people in Egypt about his secret life. Again and again, Abdelaziz denied it.

The polygraph said he was lying. Templeton continued until, finally, Abdelaziz asked to use the bathroom. Realising that things were not going well, the NYPD officials in the room tried to smooth things over with Templeton. They offered him explanations for why Abdelaziz might have seemed deceitful. But when Abdelaziz returned from the bathroom, tension remained. As Templeton delved into Abdelaziz's past, the NYPD abruptly ended the test. It was an embarrassing moment. The department's prized informant was apparently lying. The FBI closed the file as 'Deceptive with no admissions, interrupted and terminated by the NYPD'. The FBI severed its relationship with Abdelaziz, and the government tried unsuccessfully to deport him.

America. The land of opportunity.

This is who Khabib has now brought on board to turn his name into millions, when his talent alone should do that for him. A penny for Dana White's thoughts. But then, such figures around his organisation now mean nothing.

As Khabib and his team disappear out of sight, White interjects. 'This is awkward,' he says and, like at no other sporting event, he takes over the press conference. Can you imagine Gianni Infantino before a World Cup final alone and fielding queries because Didier Deschamps left and Zlatko Dalić hadn't made it yet? But this is the norm here, just like the step of allowing fans into the press conference.

Soon, he's back to excusing the cause of this waste of everyone's time. 'Listen, this shit happens.' And he laughs off a query about consequences for McGregor for a breach of contractual obligations. He even finds time to refer to a female journalist as 'honey'. The crowd are loving it.

Then, on the big screen, as if timed, there's a shot of McGregor entering the building in an Irish cap and a sleeveless T-shirt that would have done Rab C. Nesbitt proud. Clutching a bottle of Proper 12, he emerges onto stage with a walk built solely to project power when, to trained observers, it is an insight into self-doubt. He hands White the whiskey. The crowd go wild, as if the zenith of their being is for others to hear their screamed adoration.

'What's up, Ireland? The Irish are back in town, I fucking love it. The traffic is heavy out there, you know yourself.' It feels scripted, nervous, staged, and slightly desperate, like a lad in the school talent show who opted for a comedy routine only to realise once on stage that he's not all that funny.

But silence is the great enemy at these gigs, so he's now off on one.

'He knew what he fucking signed up for; I've been later than this,' he shouts, working the room and himself. 'The traffic is a little bit heavy, there must be a McGregor fight going on. I don't know where the little fool is. He's better off running. I bet he was up here saying a load of shit. He didn't say anything the last time. So whatever. It is what it is. Fuck it. I'm only a couple of fucking minutes late. The mad, backwards cunt, he should have just stayed put. He doesn't want to be around me. He doesn't want to be around these people. He is petrified. Fuck it. I've given ye enough bleeding face-offs and shit. He has to make weight, make sure he gets that fucking weight off him. So get that man into the sauna and cook him like the little chicken-jawed rat that he is. Now, who's on the Proper whiskey? I plan on knockin' that man's nose straight into the nose bleeds.'

The Irish have a reputation here, and whether it was ever as the isle of saints and scholars is debatable. But a wander around the Park MGM confirms that, even if it was, it is not anymore. These people help make McGregor what he is, telling him he can do no wrong no matter what wrong he does. They accept and celebrate whatever limit he takes his conversation to, and abuse those that try and tell them it went too far, always bringing the bar with them no matter how low it all goes.

It's the widespread acceptance of this behaviour that has allowed him to exploit it with an act so obvious that it's embarrassing people don't get it.

White, too, glances down on this with a smile, like a proud father having a moment with his son.

'You should never take information from an informant,' McGregor continues. He's returned to a correct but bizarre message that feels lost when he's not aiming it at anyone here. 'His manager is a fucking snitch terrorist rat. He was pulled off a flight going from Cairo, Egypt going to New York City on 11 September 2001. He was caught with five passports in his possession. He turned informant and turned on the people he was working with. I don't even know how that man is in this fucking country. It beggars belief. He's a rat bastard and I'm going to get him on Saturday night. Fuck him and his mentality. I don't give a fuck about him and his people. There is way deeper shit than just a fight on Saturday night. I am coming to put a hole in this man's skull, dint my knuckle into his orbital bone. Fuck peace. There will never be peace here.'

Some questions follow.

American journalists, for whatever reason, almost always ask the athlete to visualise some aspect. It's bizarre, although it's still a step above what an Israeli member of media has crossed the globe to query the former champion about. 'Let's talk about whiskey for one second. The crowd seems to be very pleased about that, but your whiskey hasn't arrived yet in Israel, and I wonder if it's good as in some places. In the Business Insider I read that ...' McGregor cuts off any potential criticism.

'Ask my bollocks, mate.' For once, he is amusing, but only because the journalism is so bad it actually deserves this response. 'Have a drink now and tell me what you think,' he goes on. 'There'll always be begrudgers and people that are hating, it comes with the territory when you're at the top of the game. Trust me, it is the tastiest Irish whiskey there is on the planet. I fucking love it. I'm not even trying to sell it. Just have a sip. Take a bottle of it with you and enjoy yourself.' The journalist walks towards the stage.

'No, not you,' McGregor screams at him. 'The smell of you. Keep him out of here, bringing up negative shit. You ask my bollocks mate. This is for the Irish. Here, when I count to three, I want everyone in this building to scream at the top of their lungs.'

* * *

'FUCK THE JAMESON BROTHERS,' RINGS OUT AGAIN.

An anthem for the week.

But it's also a warning: while one fighter is busy getting ready, the other is still selling a bottle of booze. With that, he's off on one in this direction, taking him further and further from where he needs to be. The numbers for Proper 12 sales are back and it's doing great, exceeding expectations. They've run out of it in some places and the only problem is keeping up with demand, but there's no worries as there's enough in Vegas.

The crowd roars as if their breath might touch against his glowing skin.

This is McGregor's church.

Granted, it's not great, even by the standard of churches.

Next, it's briefly back to Khabib.

'You just cook yourself in that sauna, you fucking smelly Dagestani rat.'

Next, he catches himself. Things happen quick at 200mph.

The strangest fleeting moment occurs.

It's as if the mask suddenly slips and the parody subsides, and you realise the old him is still buried in there somewhere, like Darth Vader with his real face on show right before his passing. A shard of sun breaking through a threatening sky. 'Thank you so much, truly, from the bottom of my heart,' he tells the fans. At a time and in a place when the entire concept of the Me Too movement is on show and fighting for its life, so much of McGregor can be about Me Only. Yet here he is, thanking White for what he has done with and for the UFC, thanking his management for the money he has made, thanking the fans for again following him here in droves.

For a split second, it's like being back in McDonald's on Dublin's Long Mile Road in 2013, listening to a decent guy who was dreaming big.

Even a ludicrous question about his mental warfare having surpassed that of Muhammad Ali is beaten back down by humility, as he talks about how having his name mentioned in the same sentence is 'borderline embarrassing'.

McGregor talks a little while longer. About whether the hunger is there. About how his legacy is set. Like a man on the way down and on the way out of this chapter, rather than a man desperate to win. 'Times are good, so let's enjoy it.' The last inquiry from the floor is how long before he's a billionaire. He says 35 and says he appreciates the question.

And that's it.

Sitting here, I wonder if this is the danger of normalisation, of moving the posts due to the sheer quantity of idiocy we've so often had to endure from him, as if any flickers of light are blinding.

Trying to make sense of it all and trying to step back and see the wider picture, I get talking with Karim Zidan, a prominent MMA writer originally from Egypt. 'I was recently back home,' he says. 'In a Muslim country, we were sitting over whiskey talking about how pissed they were that McGregor shoved whiskey in his face, and for sure there's a level of hypocrisy in that. But there's a level of pride and a feeling of, "How dare he not understand this man's faith?" Muslims are very touchy about religion, in a way that Christians aren't in my experience. So maybe that wouldn't have gone off as bad in Ireland as in the Muslim world. We've seen it in the past with cartoons of the Prophet Mohammad and calls for the cartoonist to be beheaded. Nonsense like that.

'But it's known that people get very sensitive and touchy when it has something to do with Islam, so no one can be surprised by the reaction. I thought after going so hard with the political jabs, and making good points, when he's standing up and passing whiskey and calling Khabib a mad, backward cunt, that was uncalled for. It didn't add anything. If anything, it creates an anger towards McGregor. When you incite that ethnic hatred, it's very difficult for people to see your side, no matter if you have moments of humility. It is a really bad strategy. Maybe it was off the cuff and just came out, but for someone who's been so good about that kind of stuff in the past, it is a major miscalculation. I say this not as a religious person.'

Those who came to see him from a new, more confident, and hugely secular Ireland wouldn't agree. For this is their pilgrimage.

They stream out contented, their sermon over for the day.

CHAPTER 14

DEATH

FOR A SPORT BUILT ON SO MUCH EMPTY TALK, IT'S fascinating how nobody will talk about McGregor.

Sitting at a kitchen table back in Ireland, shifting from texts to emails, the replies march behind one another as if a funeral procession. Dennis Siver apologises but wants to move on from the abuse as well as the beating he endured against Conor McGregor. I'm told Nate Diaz will never respond and it's a correct assertion. Max Holloway's agent says, 'I'm pretty sure he's not gonna want to add any more to Connor's [sic] story until they fight again.' There's a telltale trend there. Eddie Alvarez sums it up as he's only interested in chatting about him if it helps him get another fight and decides that it won't. Chad Mendes's representatives are similar in their attitude.

It's all about the sell and making more within the game.

Basically no one will contribute if it involves actual honesty or if there's no chance they'll get a rematch and cheque out of it. McGregor is to be pandered to because of the potential payday he could provide for others. He has the power to change lives, so those athletes grovel. That's quite a position the kid from Crumlin has gotten himself into. He's above any and all else.

Then there's Ali Abdelaziz. The informant. The alleged double agent.

He sees a WhatsApp message but doesn't respond, so I call him to chat about the abuse he's endured. He starts screaming down the line. 'Who is this? How dare you ring me on a number I don't know.' I explain he'd know the number from the message he saw and that I'll send another message if that makes it okay. Another message is sent. He sees this one, too.

I call back immediately and he just rants some more before hanging up.

Looking at the screen as the line goes dead, his photo in the corner stands out. It's of him, in a red tweed evening jacket and purple tie, pulling a face that combines the illusion of both grandeur and danger. It's reminiscent of the weeks around the fight in Vegas, when a fake city played host to a bunch of questionable businessman acting in an unnatural way to make money from the WWE-style pre-fight promises and ramblings.

It works, too, partly because of how low the standards for the stars and their teams are. Their behaviour is usually so bad that any kind of human response is deemed great, and that was the feeling after the end of the press conference in October. Just ask yourself why it's important to fans that these are accessible people. It's because it helps them to hold onto the notion that one day, they'll be able to befriend them somehow. They want to hang on to their fantasy, like a stalker with a woman he has never met.

Thankfully, Dublin is not like any of that if you know how to steer clear of the new money of bankers, traders, and tech employees. There's February rain instead of Nevada sun today; a howling winter wind instead of a deathly calm in the air; the path in Blanchardstown is overgrown rather than perfectly manicured via plastic grass or by grim jobs held by immigrants with nail clippers. There's dog shit right in the middle.

Vegas may boast a vulgarity akin to Wall Street, a falsity of Singapore, and a copy-cat streak of Dubai. But Dublin has a heart. There's something earthy and alive in that. Maybe that's why McGregor keeps coming back.

Maybe it's something else.

Boxing is comparable in that regard, too. Mixed martial arts may like to think of itself as a brother, but if so, then it's the obnoxious young sibling who may have less money but still flaunts it more loudly. It's why there's never been the historical portrayal of UFC that boxing is so celebrated for, because there's only access to the promo and to the carefully constructed lies and lines. Look at how differently boxing tends to be in its interactions. The sweet science has always had an open door, possibly because fighters have to sell themselves and their bouts. That's real. More and more, UFC fighters seem to be all front.

Paschal Collins comes from a boxing family, and I'm here in this suburb in the north of Dublin to meet him. He's a world away from those show-time pseudo-gangsters that manage their UFC fighters while going through life always muttering beside every decision, 'What's in it for me?' As he orders up two coffees, Collins starts telling true stories that aren't manufactured and marketed to be more valuable.

For instance, his brother Steve travelled to the States in the 1980s, and he followed him there. 'We wanted to be successful so maybe we could come home and buy a house. You had to do it in cash, as there was twenty percent mortgages. Ireland was awful. This was the only way.' In Boston, he remembers picking up a journalist one day, but as he drove him in a banged-up second-hand car he'd gotten dirt cheap, two things happened. The heavens opened and the windscreen wipers stopped working. So Collins came up with an ingenious solution. He tied both his shoelaces to the wipers, had the journalist sit behind him in the back and pull on the strings. They hit the freeway and got on with it.

If that had ever happened to the ilk of Abdelaziz, it would've been hidden away in shame.

The Collinses kept on at it out there for a while before making it home. By 1994, Steve was a world champion and by 1995, he famously fought Chris Eubank in Millstreet. Another brother, Roddy, was a football manager in Northern Ireland. With one of his team's games finishing late afternoon on the same day as his brother's big night, he found himself having to get from one end of the island to the other in a matter of hours. It was a race against the clock. He was always the Del Boy of the clan. 'I booked a private airplane from Newtownards to Farranfore,' he previously told me of the experience. 'I timed it. The match was over 4.45, so I got straight into a car, parked at 5.30, get to the arena 8.30. Epic. Paid over £1,200. Sterling. We arrived at the airfield, there was this contraption like a Robin Reliant with two wings sticking out of it. I was expecting something like a government jet. Fuck sake. He took off in this yoke and it was like Dam Busters. The wiper kept skipping a beat. Anyway, we got there, the greatest night of my life. Pride.'

For that to be a worthwhile tale in UFC, there'd have had to have been a Gulfstream.

But the Collinses remind me that the greatest memories often come before the money does. It's like a throwback to when you'd drink cheap cans at home during college and sneak into a club with a bottle of vodka, and have more laughs then than during any of the more grand and expensive nights later on. And Paschal, who runs a gym here, remembers when McGregor was like that, too. Not a penny to lose but a dream to gain. The most wonderful of intersections, even if you don't know it at that very moment.

It was 2012 and Collins knew little about MMA. That was about to change.

Recently, Paschal has been watching a documentary about Hollywood legends and heard them talk about Robert Redford. 'They said that when he walked into the room even as a young man, you'd notice him,' he smiles. 'It was like an event, and he just stood out. They said there was just this air of confidence about him. There are so many fighters that come in and out of the gym – boxing, Thai boxing and MMA too more recently. But when Conor walked in – even the way he was groomed, he had the skinhead – he looked really, really healthy; there was this shine from that. And looking at him, I knew he took care of himself. His skin was clear, you knew he ate well and drank well. His physique was unbelievable. I didn't know him personally but straight away, he caught my eye.

'He started to work and, funny enough, he had good boxing skill, so I thought that's why he was coming into me. A bit of work and this kid could go somewhere. But a few lads told me he was Cage Rage champion or one of these MMA things based here. Fair play, I thought. And he was likeable. He was genuine. He knew what he wanted. He wouldn't bother you, but he'd ask a question politely. And what I liked, if he came over and asked something and got his answer, he'd go off and be practicing what I told him. He picked up on every little thing, every detail. Then you wouldn't see him for a month, and he'd be back and then he'd go, and you'd get a text that would ask if he could come to the gym at night. I never watched UFC before him, but I heard he had a big win in Sweden. And maybe if that hadn't have happened we wouldn't be here talking. But that was a huge win, and I saw all the media outlets in Ireland talking about him, so I gave it a look and got into it.'

His early memories of the Conor McGregor that nobody knew? The kid came into his gym one day, and he was just inside the door, buck naked, changing into sweats, without a care in the world. There were others there sniggering, but that didn't matter as he was there for one mission and it was about dragging himself to the top.

'Sometimes, he'd come over to the gym for spars and he'd spar anybody,' continues Collins. 'He'd spar my nephew, who is a cruiserweight. Light-welterweights too, middleweights, the lot. Then he'd do some pads. It was a case of who he fought. If it was someone that required his striking to be brought to the next level, he'd be here. But it's funny, you wouldn't see him for a couple of months, but when he'd come back, you'd see a different style around how he'd box. One time, I hadn't seen him, and he came back and his stance was similar, but he was throwing punches from above his head, like a hammer, and I was looking at this and thinking it's so odd. But it was effective, because my guy would come back to the corner and say it's weird, and we couldn't figure it out.

'I spoke to Conor after, and he said it's a move from Shotokan [a style of karate] and he'd been doing that as well. I took from that myself. Sometimes, in close, it's a good shot and it's not illegal so long as you hit with the front of his hand. My brother Steve, when he was fighting, picked up some kung fu from Tony Quinn and a lot of his stances later in his career came from that. It reminded me of him, and Conor is a guy that wants to learn. He's very intelligent, and the most important part of any athlete is that, to have a brain, because you can't teach someone that doesn't want to be taught. A lot of his success is the ground work and learning he has done himself. Even when I saw him first, six or seven years ago, he was a hard trainer sure, but he was a clever trainer. He'd maybe go at six in the morning and again at three, and he'd train again eleven at night. So he was doing then what a lot of high-performance athletes still hadn't started yet. He was way ahead of his time.'

Curious about him and his looks, Collins sought Conor out on another one of his visits to the gym to ask him about his diet, and he was met with a chef's reply. He'd never heard of putting almond butter on chicken before but McGregor lectured about the good fats mixed with protein and how it tasted nice. A maverick of sorts.

'So even before he got to the stage of the UFC, he was giving it his all, from his diet to his training to the time he put into the game to his educating himself. It wasn't like he was in the gym all the time, but when he was there, he was there to learn, was very respectful, and went off and did his own thing. Nobody bothered him, because he was there to train. And it goes back to what I said about Steve in the 80s. He was a hungrier fighter and there was nothing here at that time. He was hungry to make something of himself. Conor was exactly like that; he was desperate to get out of here and be somebody.

'Do I think he's made mistakes since? Yes. We all do, but he's in the public eye, so when he makes them, they are out there. I've made mistakes, you've made mistakes, but they pass by. Not for him. Remember he's human, though. I've met his partners in the whiskey, clever businessmen. I don't know his agent, but I believe he is clever. And John's [Kavanagh] influence might help him through these tough times. And they are tough times, people forget that, because people want to take from you. They'll accuse you of everything. I've seen it with Steve. They want you to crash into them, I've seen people say, "Hit me," because they want to take money. That's the downside of having too much wealth.'

Behind it, though, he says there are still glimpses of the old McGregor there. For instance, a week after the Khabib fight, the two would meet in Boston at the Katie Taylor bout when his entourage weren't around. Ringside, they got shooting the breeze. 'We sat there and talked about acquaintances we both have that used to box with me, and he enjoyed it. Simple things, and he had a laugh. You could see he enjoyed it. The promoters took him away, and he came back and I got a text the next day saying, "Great catching up, I'll see you in the gym soon," and I was kind of glad of that as it was still him. Six years ago, he had nothing, and now he's one of the most popular and wealthiest stars of this generation.

'And deep down, you are still the person your parents brought you up to be. Fame can change you a bit and that shows sometimes as he makes silly little mistakes, but I know when Conor comes back to the gym, he'll sit on the couch and take off his clothes and won't care. That side won't change. I was over in SBG before Christmas, I had a heavyweight sparring, and Conor was cageside shouting instructions to his fighter, and it was getting a little heated, because that's him and that's the way he is. It doesn't matter if he's worth €150 or €150 million, that's just the way he is, and he's still being himself.'

I ask him what is next, and Collins suggests Dublin is too small for McGregor.

I ask him about McGregor's career, having not won a match since 2016, and he talks about how fighters find it tough to get out.

'The one thing you miss is being in the ring in front of all these people. That buzz you can't get. If you have twenty fights in the cage, you've experienced that roar and atmosphere and danger, and not knowing if you'll win or lose. You have that twenty times in your life, that's the best part. The training is the problem. But the buzz is electric. When the fight is over, it's not the money but the buzz they miss. A coach will say, "You're past it, you'll get hurt, go out on a high." When I stopped boxing, I got back into horse riding, I love the buzz of jumping fences. I got my buzz somewhere else. So, I think he loves the buzz and that makes him come back. The one thing about Conor is that he's brave, lots of courage; he's not scared of losing.'

Whether that's a positive or negative remains to be seen, for so many stories in this sphere have so many grotesque endings. McGregor knows it, even if he doesn't want to.

* * *

ACROSS THE CITY, THE NATIONAL BOXING ARENA IS tucked into the largely residential street that is the South Circular Road. You'd drive right past the understated facade if it wasn't for the signs outside for bingo a few nights of the week. That's usually its main purpose, even if it is the home of Irish amateur boxing and a place the perfect size for smaller shows.

Total Extreme Fighting decided to have an MMA event there on 9 April 2016.

McGregor was present to support his friend Charlie Ward, who came with a brutal reputation. As John Kavanagh had said of him before, 'We gave him the nickname "The Hospital Ward". I think that's quite fitting. There are some fighters that you might face where you might get submitted, there are some fighters that you go up against where you might get knocked out clean, but if you're going to fight Charlie, you're going to leave that fight hurt. There's no two ways of saying it. You might have to go to the hospital ward. I like that nickname a lot. Charlie is not too fond of it, but I'm going to throw it out there and see if it catches.' It was sadly and terrifyingly prophetic.

His opponent that night in 2016 was a Portuguese fighter by the name of João Carvalho. With just a few months in age on McGregor and a similar dream as him, this was still distinctly small time. For instance, at the time MMA wasn't even recognised by Sport Ireland, meaning it was self-policed. Many had warned of the dangers. Less than two weeks before that bout, Professor Dan Healy, a consultant neurologist at Beaumont Hospital and the Royal College of Surgeons in Dublin, wrote an article in the *Sunday Independent* complaining about the conflict of interest in such a situation. Safety costs, but promoters are there to make money, thus one plus one doesn't get you to three.

For a few years, Healy, along with McGregor's old teammate Aisling Daly, had tried to introduce the notion of a Safe MMA event, where those behind it must sign up to a fighter passport. Obtaining one involved a yearly medical, semi-annual blood tests, pre and post-fight medicals, a confidential database for competitors' well-being and current medical status, member promotions only using athletes found within the registered database, listed promotions upholding medically advised suspensions, access to specially negotiated rates for blood tests and MRI scans, and access to sports-based medical advice that fighters can trust. All of that would come too late for Carvalho.

Up close to the octagon, McGregor and others will have seen the beating he took. By the end of the first round, there was the river of blood streaming from the Portuguese's nose, but that's nothing unusual in what, at times, can seem a sport better fitted to some terrible Steven Seagal post-apocalyptic action movie. By round three, the referee had to step in, with Ward towering over his defenceless opponent throwing a stream of fists to his face. Again, nothing unusual in this realm.

After a few moments, Carvalho was able to walk back to the medical room under his own power, and the card went on. There were no immediate symptoms as the doctor ran a few normal tests and found nothing out of the ordinary in the results. Crucially, though, he recommend a CT scan, and an ambulance was called to take Carvalho to hospital as a precaution. It was there that matters deteriorated. A headache flared up; he began throwing up violently. The hospital was informed in advance that a serious case was now on the way. Emergency surgery followed. Carvalho was kept on life support for 48 hours, but nothing could be done. By Monday at 9.35pm, a switch was flicked and life support was turned off.

Cesar Silva, the promoter of Total Extreme Fighting, took no responsibility for what happened, and there was no insurance written into it, even if the initial idea of money around a death can seem like no more than a pillow on the ground for a sky-high jump.

A post-mortem examination, carried out by state pathologist Dr Marie Cassidy, found that Carvalho died from an acute subdural haemorrhage due to blunt force trauma to the head. In layman's terms, it was a blood clot.

Quickly, a debate began, his corpse used as a flashpoint for anger. *Irish Times* sports writer Malachy Clerkin nailed it in a piece published shortly after: 'His death made the news across the world. His life was barely mentioned. Instead, he became a cypher. A battleground state. Weaponised by ban-it-all fundamentalists on one side, deified by watery-eyed MMA soldiers on the other. He could have been anybody. The world of mixed martial arts was always going to be one punch away from a moment of reckoning and he was just the poor schmoe who took it. It was, literally, nothing personal. But João Carvalho was somebody. And was from somewhere. He had a family and he had a wife and he had kids. He had friends and a job and bad habits and a sense of humour and nickname. He had good times and tough times, he had ambitions and he had heroes.'

Such a tragedy will have many victims at many levels. Clerkin was right to pay homage to the damage done to those most affected – namely Carvalho, his family, and his friends. But what about McGregor looking on at that, too? A pilot witnessing a plane crash is bound to be a different person the next time they take a seat in the cockpit.

In this area, there are many examples of what such horrific moments can do, not just to the person physically hurt, for that hurt leaves a trail of psychological damage spread far and wide. For instance, Chris Eubank had seventeen stoppage wins in his 28 fights before he fought Michael Watson in 1991 in a brutal battle that was more akin to a bout-scene from a Rocky film. Round after round, they stood toe-to-toe, trading, before he finally knocked out his countryman. Watson's life was changed forever by the brain damage inflicted upon him in the ring, but it of course changed Eubank in a big way too. As a person, but also in his profession. Thereafter, at times, he begged referees to step in instead of landing another punch to a battered human being on their last legs.

In Donald McRae's book *Dark Trade*, he goes back over several interviews he did when spending time with Eubank after the night that put Watson in a coma for forty days due to a blood clot, and you could see how it altered his style. After the pre-fight war of words, he explained why he always referred to the man he beat up by his full name. His rationale was that it recognised him as a whole, complete person rather than what was left after they fought.

'Before our second fight,' he noted, 'I said things about Michael Watson, things I now regret. I said Michael Watson was transparent, that he was nothing. How wrong could I be? Michael Watson was a superman that night – but, in the end, his humanity took over. He was just human at the end – a man whose life has been destroyed.'

Shortly after, he was explaining why he himself would go on in that game, as if justification was needed. Another hat tip to how his own outlook was shifted clean off its axis. 'I, like Michael Watson, am a fighter. This is my trade, and I will continue to box as long as my economic circumstances dictate that this is necessary. I have to fight until I have enough money. My heart is with Michael Watson, but it will not help him for me to give up my living. I've said this to people – they cannot know how sorry I am for Michael, how sorry I am for the mother, how sorry I am for the man's family and friends. But allow me to live with my sorrow, allow me to continue my business, allow me to be a businessman, too.'

He went on to say he'd give everything up in terms of his wealth to give Watson back his health. Recalling what happened in the ring, he said, 'I think that this is a horrible business. Punching another man in the head with the force of two tons of pressure. I think that makes this a heavy business. I think that there's dark shit in boxing.'

* * *

MCGREGOR DIDN'T DIRECTLY INFLICT THE ACCIDENT

that happened to João Carvalho, but there's no way it didn't make him aware of the damage he could do. Or, worse, the damage that could be done to him. That doesn't leave you. For all his bravado, there's no escaping that.

Afterwards, he was quick to release a statement, and the words were more than mere box-ticking. 'To see a young man doing what he loves, competing for a chance at a better life, and then to have it taken away is truly heartbreaking,' he wrote. 'We are just men and women doing something we love in the hope of a better life for ourselves and our families. Nobody involved in combat sports of any kind wants to see this. It is such a rare occurrence that I don't know how to take this. I was ringside supporting my teammate, and the fight was so back and forth, that I just can't understand it.

'My condolences go out to João's family and team. Their man was a hell of a fighter and will be sorely missed by all. Combat sport is a crazy game and with the recent incident in boxing and now this in MMA, it is a sad time to be a fighter and a fight fan. It is easy for those on the outside to criticise our way of living, but for the millions of people around the world who have had their lives, their health, their fitness and their mental strength all changed for the better through combat, this is truly a bitter pill to swallow. We have lost one of us. I hope we remember João as a champion, who pursued his dream doing what he loved, and show him the eternal respect and admiration he deserves.

Rest in peace, João.'

What it leaves is a tug-of-war you can't win between the buzz and the danger.

Maybe that's why, at times, McGregor seems to be fighting himself. In Vegas, at the end of his rambling press conference, it was like a farewell, and the fight itself didn't involve the fearless and ferocious fighter we had got used to. No longer in need of the pay cheque, was that one more reason to not care, to take less of the risk, to not go all in?

Tapping out before more real damage could be done.

Because this isn't like a track athlete retiring. This is putting your health on the line for a thrill.

It's not uncommon for top fighters to struggle to let go, though. A couple of years back, Roy Jones and Steve Collins talked about a fight we wanted in a different millennium. In December 2016, Bernard Hopkins got into the ring aged 51 and was literally punched out of it. In fact, in terms of not accepting the difference between past and present, a story from 1997 sums it up. After being stopped by Naseem Hamed in their featherweight title fight, journalist Paul Howard saw Tom 'Boom Boom' Johnson in a hotel lobby and approached him. The American said the result was a sign from God, the presumption being he should retire. But after pausing, he added, 'I should move up to lightweight.'

That yearning for more makes sense. You don't want to let go of the past because you don't know how to fill the rush into the future. It's like admitting that what made you great is over, and you step into a void you'll likely never fill in the same way. When your life hits a summit, it's downhill from there.

Back in Blanchardstown, Collins thinks the next phase for McGregor will be the movies. 'I think he and his partner and kids should move off to LA and do their time, as there would be like-minded people and celebrities who get where he is, and they can help him. People who've been there and know how to handle all this. He's a clever guy. But first I think there'll be Khabib again, Diaz again, and Malignaggi in the ring.'

That he has options doesn't mean he'll make the right choice, but at least he has that choice. Others didn't. In the neighbourhood of Lisbon, where João Carvalho was from, there's a mural that reads, *'Antes morrer lutando do que viver fugindo.'*

It's better to die fighting than to live running away.

Perhaps.

CHAPTER 15

SHOWTIME

FOR A WHILE NOW, WHEN THE PHONE RINGS AND the person on the other end asks if I heard about Conor McGregor, I've assumed the worst. That's not meant as attention-seeking through overstatement, rather it's a link to his lifestyle of late. He can give the perception that he has stopped being a serious sportsman, instead morphing into some sort of full-time celebrity; a kind of male Kim Kardashian. And, given how often he's in the news, you'd be surprised at how many of those calls there've been.

From friends.

From editors.

From radio stations.

From television.

The business end shows how important he's become in a modern era of media: it's in their interests to keep him front and centre, because he generates the clicks that make their ads more valuable. It's mutually beneficial to all from a financial perspective, but in reality it reduces standards each time, often in terms of both him and journalism.

At times, there's a sad logic to some of his behaviour no matter how repulsive it has become. This is a man loved by millions but often overwhelmed by a handful — on the one hand trying to shout away the vacuum, on the other trying escape the noise.

There can be no balance.

This morning, though, as the phone rings in my Vegas hotel room, even though it's the day of the fight, there's no worry around McGregor. It's strange how such a violent job is his salvation from himself. On the other line are the two journalists I was out with last night. While I had come home at about 3am, they had kept going. 'You don't have a spare laptop?' one asks.

I try not to laugh but fail.

It turns out that, sitting at a bar further on into the morning, unknown to themselves, two prostitutes took the chairs beside them. Receiving no attention, the women decided to get something for their efforts, so they grabbed their bags and meandered out the door. It wasn't just the computers but their credit cards and, even worse, their passports. Staff looked at security footage, recognised the women, and made some calls. The pair were told they wouldn't be working there again if the goods weren't returned, and soon they were. Minus the laptops, which the two of them hung onto as a tip for their troubles.

At this point, with the clock nearing breakfast time, one of the journalists decided to celebrate getting back his belongings with an array of shots and cocktails, and was soon found asleep in a hall outside someone else's room. Carried back to his own by members of staff and waking up with a sore body as well as a pounding head, he bemoaned why they sat him in a chair rather than throwing him onto his bed. If that sounds extreme, then you need to be here for Vegas can easily get the better of you — and quickly, too. It claws at the senses to the point of making them raw and eventually numb to its madness. It even closes the chasm between those here to cheer and those here to cover McGregor. Like so many present here, McGregor-ised in McGregorland.

And yet somewhere in the midst of all this madness, he himself was like a man right before walking down the green mile. There can be no greater contrast in all of sports than when big bouts come to this place. Calm planning in the midst of lunacy. Living in the moment as he plans for *the* moment. So how did he sleep? So what did he think?

With the ticking getting louder, does he ever question why he does this?

To be a fly on the wall.

When he fights, here is the pond the stone is thrown into, but there are ripples that emanate right around the globe. In Brazil, if you mention you are Irish, his is the name that comes up. In Australia, a friend who works for the Melbourne police force hates when McGregor's in action as, due to the time difference, bars are worked into a frenzy across sunrise, with those dressed like him getting a high from his ego, his antics, and his violence. This friend tells me that back when he used to win, most locals were only waking up but the transplanted Irish were often already topless, spilling out onto the streets, looking for a dust-up with anyone.

It's the ultimate way to mimic what he had done so well.

But on the edge of destiny in Vegas, suddenly it's different.

More professional. More nervous. More real.

The fun is over.

Outside the T-Mobile Arena, you can get a sense of how the UFC has grown in the 25 years since its inception as an obscure carnival act, and you get a sense of how McGregor can command the talk of so many looking to be entertained, despite so many other options dotted all around. Only a mere blink ago, in his small and oft forgotten suburb of Dublin, he was an unknown nobody. Now, that makes this feeling of vertigo hard to fathom.

The fans are a little better behaved today, but that wouldn't be hard.

Twenty-four hours ago, at the weigh-in across the road, McGregor and Khabib Nurmagomedov got in each others' faces as expected, with the Russian refusing to flinch. It was all too much for some knuckle-draggers, though, with heads turning away from the commotion on stage as, for whatever reason, punches started flying between both men and women in the audience.

It felt like some bravado on their parts gone wrong, that their mouths had written a cheque they could not cash. Now that it's getting real, is there a comparison to be made with McGregor? All those insults he launched no longer matter. Strip away the talk and the attitude, and suddenly he's faced with a man who is superior, faced with his own demons and doubts, allied to a body that hasn't done this lately.

Looking for signs, a little drizzle kicks in briefly, providing that wonderful release of heat so long trapped in the concrete ground and that wonderful smell of damp on dust. What does it mean? Likely nothing, but it doesn't stop some claiming that it does. 'We've even managed to bring the weather with us to Nevada,' laughs one Irish person. 'Bodes well,' they smile.

Inside, there's the stale waft of air conditioning, and a labyrinth of stairs and confused employees when it comes to finding the press area. Or at least the secondary press area. The UFC, always looking for more money, have sold half the seats in what was the media pen at cageside, for massive prices, meaning many of us are forced into the rafters.

So be it. While some complain, they are getting a memory to look back on for a long time.

The friend who was found on the floor of the hotel hall just a few hours ago arrives the worse for wear, his green skin and epic shakes accompanied by a mutter.

'What was I thinking?'

As in the morning, I try not to laugh. As in the morning, I fail.

But he's doing just fine compared to Jalin Turner down below in the cage. So bad is the beating he's allowed to take from Vicente Luque in their undercard welterweight clash that there's a moment that involves a contemplation of humanity and of the notion of sitting watching this. The Brazilian forced his opponent to the canvas and proceeded to beat an initially defenceless and then unconscious man with a series of vicious overhand lefts. There was time for the official to dive in sooner, but — as is so often the case in UFC to the point you wonder if it's intentional — the referee lets it go on for those extra and lethal few seconds.

Bang. Bang. Bang. Bang.

There's a momentary flashback to being in my hometown of Athy many years ago. With two schools as rivals in the small south Kildare settlement, one lunchtime down the river a huge crowd gathered as a pupil from each were going to go at it. We skipped food and ran down filled with excitement, but there's always been that lasting, fleking sound of a skull hitting the pavement after a punch, and that was it. We walked away feeling sickly. Here, though, when one bounces off the canvas, it goes on, and those watching scream approval.

Turner takes a number of minutes to come around, and when he does, his first attempt to get to his feet sees him fall back over. The crowd love it. It appeals to both their funny bone and blood-thirsty streak. Another story for their buck. As for Turner, he will later be given $10,000 and a handshake for this battering. It's why so many from Duran to Malinaggi abhor this event, and why McGregor upon entering refused to play by their exploitative upstairs-downstairs rules.

Meanwhile, backstage, the fight is on the television screens dotting the tunnels and rooms. And this might be what awaits the Dubliner. What does he think?

With the ticking getting louder, does he ever question why he does this?

Salvation, maybe.

The lesser of two evils.

Funny, the things that keep a man sane.

I go for a coffee.

During this break from what I've just witnessed, a debate rages in my head about what's taking place here. How much do you interfere with people before it becomes big brother and nanny-state stuff? During its rise, UFC supporters riled against that sort of dictatorial tut-tutting. Those who don't like it don't have to watch it and, if the brutality can come across as grotesque in even calm moments, does that have to be a personal choice?

Either way, what a choice.

* * *

BY NOW, IT'S LIKE I'M TRYING TO CONVINCE MYSELF that it's okay to return to my seat and watch some more. To help this process along before getting back to work, I recall a conversation struck up not long before. It was with Dr Willie Stewart, a consultant neuropathologist at Glasgow's Southern General Hospital. For many years, Stewart has studied the effects of Chronic Traumatic Encephalopathy, once, and perhaps more strikingly, known as punch-drunk syndrome.

'In the past, concussion was thought of as your brain misfiring and then going back to normal, but it's clear at a cellular level [that] your brain has been damaged,' he had explained. 'It's not the kind of damage that would show up on a brain scan, but it is the damage that, if I get a person's brain, I can see it down a microscope. The fine fibres, or cables, that connect all the parts of your brain and let messages flow freely, become stretched and damaged. They no longer pass a message as quickly as they should. So your brain is trying to get you to stand, but the message isn't getting to your legs. Or you're trying to remember [something] but just can't. And the brain isn't a good organ for healing. Cumulatively, if you have several of these injuries on top of each other, it's not just permanent damage. It's damage that gets worse, so your brain degenerates, and that leads to memory loss, headaches, personality change. What we don't know is how many might be affected.'

He wasn't talking about mixed martial arts, though.

He was talking about rugby.

This is a problem when judging MMA with the eye test rather than the medical test. Many have been brought to this place I'm now in. However, when it comes to athletes putting their bodies on the line, and when it comes to medical science, to be emotive is to be unfair and involves a degree of flat-earth methodology. So instead, with MMA, why not take a look at the truth before generalisations and allegations? What looks bad isn't always that bad and what seems brutal can be based on it being new and unfamiliar. We are used to other sports that do damage, so we give them a pass. Aside from rugby, take boxing as another example of our misplaced opinions: where is the criticism there?

If you are to go after MMA, the sweet science ought to jump to the head of that queue. There are limited studies to contrast the two given MMA is relatively new to centre stage, but there are studies nonetheless. One, from 2010, looked at the Manuel Velazquez Boxing Fatality Collection that found 339 deaths from head injuries in boxing matches from 1950 to 2007. MMA listed eight deaths surrounding the sport from 1998 to 2013.

In 2014, a separate study showed that while the probability of an injury in an MMA contest was around 22 percent, in pro boxing, it ranged from 12 percent to 25 percent. Crucial here, though, is the type of injury. Back in 2015, data showed that while MMA has that higher general risk of injury, head injuries are more likely in both boxing and also karate. In addition to that boxing has a higher rate of concussion, with 14 percent of injuries involving this form of brain damage against just four percent of MMA injuries.

In essence, while boxing is less likely to see the sort of mechanical injuries you get in the octagon, serious brain trauma is more common.

That much was expressed in a 2015 paper by Dr Shelby Karpman from the University of Alberta, as pro boxers were significantly more likely to suffer severe injuries such as retinal detachment and were nearly twice as likely to be hurt to the point of unconsciousness. This makes common sense: there are various types of submission in MMA, the fights are shorter, you cannot come back from a refereeing intervention and then there's the gear that is worn. After all, the bigger gloves in boxing aren't meant to protect the head but the hands. As a result, a one-off punch is unlikely to end it, thus allowing for a plethora of blows causing accumulative trauma. Indeed, while the padding on gloves reduces soft tissue injuries, it does little to prevent brain damage.

So should you be more repulsed by blood or by that?

It's funny how many people instinctively react to the former, as it's far more visual.

* * *

COFFEE GONE, I PULL MYSELF TOGETHER AND GO back out into the media seats.

Even if I don't like what I see, ultimately it still gives me a tingle and reminds me that in all of us, there is the most basic animalistic urge that can be fed by this.

When McGregor goes up on the big screen in his changing room, getting ready, the arena shakes. Hairs on arms stand to attention. For all he's done that I've hated, I actually feel nervous for him. Gone is that loud-mouthed facade. Maybe it's just focus, but there's no madness. Without it, he looks almost like a child. Turns out the devil is a liar.

To be in his bare feet for just a split second. The rush. The adrenaline. The fear.

How many of us will ever feel that?

How many of us would ever want to feel that?

It's hard to know what to make of the undercard. Like Vegas itself, it leaves you with so many emotions but all in very different, confusing, and contrasting ways. The fans get restless when there are tactical bouts, yet they love heavyweight Derrick Lewis and his all-swinging style that means he'll either flatten a guy or get beaten up. There's little skill to this. Losing, with eleven seconds left and badly out-of-breath, he lands a haymaker of a right and soon finishes the dazed and defenceless Alexander Volkov on the canvas.

For some reason, he then leaps to his feet and takes off his trunks.

When asked why he did it, he says his 'balls were hot'.

It would be baffling if you didn't realise that McGregor has been a crusader and they all want to go low to get noticed, in the hope of getting more attention, bigger fights, and bigger paydays. It's the new UFC way.

Soon after, Lewis's words are replaced by the action between Tony Ferguson and Anthony Pettis. By round two, as the latter lies on top, the former's face is covered in such a sea of blood that there's confusion as to what happened him for a moment. Then, as the referee asks for the doctor, it becomes clear that it's Pettis's blood that has soaked his opponent's face. 'This can't be that bad that they have to stop this. It's in the hairline, a giant cut,' the commentary team beam. Across the ring, Ferguson doesn't get his face cleaned during the break, and instead smiles like a cross between a serial killer and a lion pulling his red-soaked mane from the carcass of its fallen prey for just a brief moment. His teeth and eyes are all that remain of him. The rest, including any sort of evolution, has long since been submerged.

'This is amazing,' add the commentators. It's a strange choice of word for something so terrifyingly and gloriously primal. The fight is cut short, though, as Pettis can take no more and doesn't come out for round three. The crowd boo despite having been given what they want. Some people will never be pleased.

There's little time for contemplation, though.

It's main-event time.

McGregor is out first. As the smoke from the machines clears, the canvas is stained in the claret of what went before: a reminder of what might follow, as if he wasn't already aware of this maniac profession.

It feels different to his previous bouts. John Kavanagh didn't make his usual prediction of glory. Maybe he too has been wondering what Conor's goals are now, when before it was to be a two-weight world champion and make $10m. Of late, his business dreams consume him, but what about the sporting dreams? And what about the body? Some will say he's not old, but in this arena age isn't just about a number, rather miles on the clock, via the lifestyle led, and the effects of the moments on the journey to this point.

Khabib is second in. His shoulders, his brow, and his walk suggests the pageantry is an unnecessary and bothersome distraction from what he's been yearning to do for so long. He's hunched, like a farmer heading to the fields for a day's work and with a job to get done. He doesn't so much as touch gloves, such are the words he has endured.

Now he's ready to do his pent-up talking.

It begins.

There's a gladiatorial feel to all of it.

The ancient and much maligned blood sports of the Colosseum make sense.

The ring is an existential place. You can run, but you can't hide. You are there, and you are going to get hit. Unlike in boxing, where there's some odd nobility about one athlete walking to a neutral corner to save the dignity of the other they've floored, that safety net is removed here. The UFC doesn't care for nobility. Go down and it gets worse, quick.

It's not long before McGregor is down. It takes a mere 25 seconds for Khabib to get his leg; a wrestle ensues and within a minute, the Irishman's on the ground with his feet tied up. A long four minutes to survive against the best ground-and-pound artist there is.

It's exhausting. Imagine a boa constrictor that may not have the pounce and venom to kill instantly: there's the long fight as the prey tires itself out, each little mistake seeing the snake wrap itself that bit tighter to the point of no escape.

Sweaty and flustered, McGregor returns to his corner, but the second round is similar. He's supposed to be the boxer in this match-up, but his swings and efforts are a reminder of the time away and that open workout, where his punches looked slow and out of sync. Instead, it's the Russian who seems to be the better boxer, especially 22 seconds in, when a massive, wild, and wide right bursts like a firework on McGregor's cheek. The ferocity is filled with all those words Khabib has heard in the build-up. McGregor falls back.

Soon after, he's lifted off the ground and slammed back down. On this occasion, there are more than four minutes to endure on the canvas. His bearded face, growing old before us, takes a beating that brings pain rather than the mere exhaustion of before.

There is no rope-a-dope here after all the dire Ali comparisons over the years. There is no trick. There is no way out for him.

He's trapped, caught between his stubbornness and his opponent's brilliance and resulting domination. By the second bell, all that's left is to compliment him on hanging in there. There are no other positives. Few sports highlight past and present in this cruel light. A track athlete merely gets slower and a footballer merely loses on the scoreboard, yet they can still cling to when they were kings. Not here. Not during the humiliation of being physically harmed in front of so many who came to see you thrive.

Round three.

Tick tock.

McGregor's hair is now down over his face, nearly reaching his swollen eye sockets. The end is coming. Indeed, the greatest indictment of the gulf in class is that by the end of it, McGregor slumps to his stool, barely able to get back up for round four, while Khabib refuses to sit. Instead, he's counting down the seconds before he can go back for more. On this occasion, it takes two minutes before Khabib gets onto his back from behind, wrapping a forearm around his neck, and the tap out eventually comes.

Hate manifested in brute strength, but what follows is the greatest form of anger still. Winning this fight was about control. Now, all control ceases.

For a start, only the referee's presence prevents Khabib from giving his opponent an even greater battering. Wanting that bit extra is understandable. Reading his mind isn't hard. 'Where's your whiskey and Islamophobia now?' his actions growl.

But while those of us in the press seats are still wondering what to call the act of standing behind a man and squeezing his wind pipe shut with all one's might, there's another roar down below. And another.

And some screams.

It's kicking off.

If there was an inevitability about McGregor losing, this was a moment I'd planned to watch him closely. Later, there would be more words and excuses as the mask returned, but for a split second, even the most arrogant and egotistical fighter is left naked by being stopped. In that brief instant, there is a frank realisation of what has happened;

a confusion over where they are in this life; a desperation over not wanting to accept that perhaps their time at the top is up. Next is the worry about where they go from here. Low and lonely is, sadly, the best measure of a person.

But there's no chance to observe.

Looking for one more shot after the tap out can be explained away.

This can't.

Khabib hurdles the cage and goes after Dillon Danis, a grappling partner of McGregor seated ringside. Meanwhile, as he gets to his feet inside the octagon, pulling his body and soul back together, one of Khabib's team hurdles his way into the cage and punches McGregor from behind. There are few things more cowardly than coming into a ring to hit a defeated fighter who is not only unsuspecting and defenceless, but mentally and physically spent. There is no excuse, just as there has been no excuse for McGregor on many occasions. It's confusing. An eye for an eye makes the whole world blind.

So often a hate figure, no matter what he's brought upon himself, to see that happen is to feel outraged. Not even he is deserving of this. During the bout there are at least rules.

Now they've gone and set the tone for those that follow in their footsteps, throwing a match on the petrol that's been poured all around here. In the foyer, an Irish kid spits at a Dagestani and is knocked out cold by the flash of a lethal right. His jaw's taken on a new shape, and in a place where healthcare isn't cheap. Meanwhile, none of those watching to get a kick consider the longer-term consequences. Can they not imagine him, having missed his flight out while drinking soup in a hospital bed, calling his parents back in Dublin to tell them the bill is at $10,000 and counting? It's the beginning, as the fire spreads and burns everything down.

With the governor of Nevada taken away by his security detail, others don't have that option. More spats break out. There's one man unconscious on the floor of a smoothie bar and, not learning their lesson, the Irish want to retaliate rather than get away. Outside, a group of Khabib fans in papakhas are surrounded by a large barrier of police, and the McGregor fans taunting them fail to realise that the official presence isn't to protect those celebrating, but to protect others from those celebrating.

On it goes into the night.

Back in the press area, editors want extra reports, and journalists scramble as the work load goes up and up and up. This will gain attention, therefore this is good. Maybe not in the eyes of the reporter telling the story or their newsroom colleagues, but certainly from an accountants' perspective. Forget the ugly nature of the content itself. People will want to read more, and, for days, it'll generate endless stories that will provide endless clicks.

Conor McGregor won't be speaking, though. Khabib Nurmagomedov barely speaks. Instead, it's again left to Dana White, the ringmaster of this odiousness. He comes bearing numbers. The attendance was 20,034. The gate was $17,200,000. An average of $859 a person, for that?

'If you give a shit,' he says of figures headed for the bank account. And soon he's giving his take on what just transpired. 'So I saw one of Conor's guys yelling at Khabib, and he went and jumped over the octagon and went after him. Then two of Khabib's guys went into the octagon and hit Conor with some shots from behind. And then, that's it. The Nevada State Athletic Commission pulled the footage from us, and there's an investigation. They are withholding Khabib's purse, they are not withholding Conor McGregor's. Listen, being in there in the middle of this thing going on, I have to start worrying about the fans and people inside the arena. I felt if we put the belt on him in the middle of the octagon, it was going to rain. All sorts would be thrown in there from the crowd. We were lucky just getting him out of here, so that's what we tried to do …

'The way that works, Conor was one of the guys who was attacked, he refused to press charges. The guys the police did have, there were three from Khabib's team, they've been released. The guys who jumped in will never fight here. I've been working hard for eighteen years to build this sport. Some of you this is your first event. And I can promise you this is not what a mixed martial arts event is normally like. You know, when you have such an amazing event that we've worked hard to build over the last several months and it goes perfect, security was unbelievable, we had meetings with both camps, everyone signed off, everyone was cool. Nobody saw Khabib diving over … This isn't the last time guys are going to say mean things to each other, it's the fight business, it's how it works.'

We've been here before, though.

Then it gets to the crux. A rematch?

'We have to see what happens with [the] Nevada State Athletic Commission,' White replies. 'Not just the commission, there'll be fines. Can these guys get visas and get back in the country? We'll see how it plays out. I've been doing this for eighteen years, and the biggest night ever, and I couldn't be more disappointed.'

So would he change how he marketed it? 'No. I'd do the same, it's part of the story.'

Outside, fans are still beating each other. Inside, White goes off and counts his money.

Media tap away and talk into cameras.

So this is what the zenith of sport has become?

Tonight, the two journalists who called in a panic to start this sorry day don't fancy a beer. It's not so much tiredness after their previous effort, but this has been enough and the strip genuinely isn't a safe place yet. Before going, one says, 'There'll be another bout. It's too valuable. They'll be back.'

Walking home, I wonder if there was a rematch if I'd bother. And then I wonder about McGregor. 'Combat is my escape,' he's said and while that's a nice soundbite, what if it's really true?

Of course, publicly, there will now be the usual and predictable washing away of defeat with the pay cheque, and the over-the-top counting of dollars in front of a camera to show he's the real winner in this. But if that compensation and this sort of night is the getaway he has from his demons, he must reside in a very dark place few can ever envisage.

Getting back to the hotel, I never thought the overriding emotion for him would be pity.

CHAPTER 16

FIN. FOR NOW

'BREAKING NEWS …'

It seems there's always breaking news about Conor McGregor.

It's like that drip from the leaky bathroom tap as you bed down for some sleep – no matter how much you try and ignore it, it eats away until you can take no more.

Ever since he lost to Khabib back in October, he's reverted to his other self. Any internal struggle around him getting back in the octagon or doing anything constructive with his time and opportunities was defeated. The path has been chosen, and he is walking it.

Allegations made in the international media – but not repeated in Ireland and elsewhere in the EU because of the archaic laws that govern reporting in McGregor's home country and the commonality of European law that extends these restrictions beyond the country – remain unresolved.

Next, there's been a woman claiming to have had his child. Having met him during his 2017 Liverpool tear-up around the Grand National, she's doing the rounds in the tabloids. Of course, she's been paid off by them for the story, as if a pathetic reminder of the look-at-me era we live in were needed. 'We slept together,' she said. 'To be honest, there was no sleep. We were not sleeping, do you know what I mean? I told him I wasn't on nothing [contraception], and he was like "Ah, fuck it, babe."'

When did it become better to be famous for nothing than just not being famous? To be talked about for all of this kind of behaviour rather than just not being talked about?

Now, on this March day in Dublin, the news comes on the radio that McGregor has been arrested in Florida.

Social media goes crazy. Just the mention of his name acts like a black hole, sucking in those who both love and despise him in equal measure, as well as those who want no more. So common are all the whispers and rumours that it's hard to know what's true anymore, but what's heard cannot be unheard. Even in waiting for confirmation around these latest issues, presumption gnaws at patience and eats at any better judgment.

The city these days has become like one of its best-known sons who is managing to balance fame and infamy. They say it has more money therefore it's better off, but you cannot see that. Instead that rich status is like an anchor tied to once free and flighty feet, dragging down both decency and innocence. Economists natter about how a rising tide lifts all boats, forgetting that some people are in dinghies and others in yachts.

If only McGregor had known better than to follow such an ideology.

Still, there are many who keep claiming he's remained some sort of working-class hero throughout this journey, as if the only goal of those left behind ought to be to make money and flaunt it in the most vacuous and obnoxious way possible. Ironically, McGregor's attitude fits in more with the style of those same economists who say we are all winning.

'Breaking news …'

It continues on the radio. The update says that as McGregor left his Miami Beach hotel, someone wanted a photo but McGregor wasn't having it: he threw the phone to the ground, smashed it with his boot, picked up the wreck, and wandered off. It could be worse: stars are generally hounded, and sometimes so-called fans don't know when to leave them well enough alone. But because of his rap sheet, you can't help come down that bit harder on him.

John Lennon was right about a working-class hero: 'They hurt you at home and they hit you at school. They hate you if you're clever, and they despise a fool. 'Till you're so fucking crazy, you can't follow their rules. A working class-hero is something to be.' It's just that Conor McGregor is not that.

In fact, forget the hero part, even the extent of the hardship around that working-class element is dubious. His lifestyle in Crumlin? Perhaps. A four-bed house in Lucan, though? If you are going to be a sort of hardship carpetbagger, ripping off someone else's difficulty for your gain, the least you can do is use it for good. The sad part, though, is that he's desperate to overplay that type of history he didn't really have to begin with, and then takes the negative from it.

Take the video to 'Juicy', Biggie Smalls' track about his rise from drug dealing in Brooklyn to the shiny, in-your-face, bling-bling luxury of a rap god. It overstates even what is already overstated, and it's like McGregor is trying to live that life, never realising there's a large element of parody to it all. And yet it doesn't matter, because McGregor, his spiel, and the entire act that became a pseudo-reality arrived at the perfect time to be allowed.

For all he's achieved in his sport before now, due to his vision and endless effort, there's also an element of luck to it. Twenty years earlier, it wouldn't have worked, because back then, such an attitude was deemed repugnant and the UFC was a sporting footnote, struggling to stay afloat. Hopefully, in another decade, we can look back and ask, 'What were we thinking?'

Not here and now, though.

It's a world where a generation would miss three little birds pitching by their doorstep because their faces are stuck to a screen, analysing nonsense in the most basic of ways.

It was bad enough that fans used to cleanse any and all ugly truths around their idols as, via those bizarre and unhealthy parasocial relationships, they imagined some day having a chat or a beer with them if they bumped into each other by accident. That was the level of blind faith. Now, though, they want the gangster, the out-of-control loudmouth to look up to. The guy that might smash their phone, or get them pregnant, creating a connection and giving them a story to tell and a minute of fame.

It makes you wonder what became of the great sporting heroes, the ones who stood the test of decades upon decades, whose bravery and standards are more impressive and important today than when they walked at their tallest. Sadly, they've been washed away in that same tide of stupidity.

* * *

BACK IN OCTOBER 2018, JUST TEN DAYS AFTER McGregor's latest loss, the 50th anniversary of one of the most iconic moments of all sporting history came around. It reminded some who still cared of what those heroes looked like and sounded like and acted like.

It had been half a century since Tommie Smith and John Carlos took to a podium at the Mexico City Olympics, shaking the planet to its core with their Black Power salute. For most, however, the anniversary flitted by without registering, and it also went by without so much as a word from the White House. Instead, that very day, Donald Trump was on social media, calling the porn star with whom he had cheated on his wife 'horse face'.

That we shouldn't be surprised by this shows the normalisation of the standards of that presidency, but also standards that have seeped down to even relatively trivial areas like sport. This is a sphere that was never going to be immune from the decline.

In fact, some sportspeople are exploiting this, arguably none better than McGregor. There was a point, up to the Eddie Alvarez fight, where he gave out a good message in terms of belief beyond sport, around what hard work could achieve, and the importance of confidence and not letting others tell you what to do. But since then? Putting yourself in the store as an obnoxious trailblazer sees the shelves empty far, far faster.

In this climate, is it any wonder that his is the routine that works so well?

There's a queue waiting to learn from his miserable methods, and to copy them, too. Even the once-refined and seemingly religious and respectful Khabib Nurmagomedov – not that they are always bedfellows – has started to notice that his talent alone wasn't getting him his dues. So, since his October win, he's followed the Trump model or the McGregor model or the modern model. Whatever you want to call it, for essentially they are all the same.

Parody has become truth.

Before, Nurmagomedov had a blueprint, meticulously plotting a way through the rankings in order to beat everyone. That won't happen now. Instead, he's become a sorry mimic, trying to call out Floyd Mayweather so we've to revisit that boxing match-up pointlessness, while refusing to fight in his own sport until his teammates that jumped in the cage after the most recent bout are reinstated and get a pass for their own choices, their own decisions, their own actions. This after he absolved them of their thuggery by paying their fines, before getting chippy with Dana White and making demands as to his future.

It's resulted in him getting the same sort of special treatment from White as McGregor does. He won't take part in a Nevada anti-bullying campaign that would reduce his ban, allowing him to get back to work on behalf of his employers, and he's warned the UFC that if they get rid of his friends, they can cancel his contract, too. The UFC doesn't generally handle fighters being normal very well, never mind fighters giving ultimatums. But with him, they take it on the chin as they did with McGregor before. It's because Khabib is a cultural icon and someone who is truly in the top three big Muslim athletes on planet, and they realise this. It's because that makes Khabib worth a lot.

That many in the political sphere have tried to attach themselves to a winner in a mere fight and use it to promote their brand of ugly nationalism is a telling sign of today, too. For weeks after UFC 229, the commentary in Russia was that McGregor had insulted them and that this was a country's manly retribution. Yet again, politicians were acting like children. A member of Russian parliament said he had 'crushed his opponent as Russia crushes opponents on the world stage'. And so many vile people have tried to cosy up to Khabib since.

He met Vladimir Putin immediately, even though the latter tends not to have individual sit-downs with those from the Caucasus nations after numerous wars and little support there. However, the PR was too valuable before a slack-jawed audience. Putin laughed and joked, and told Khabib's father not to punish him too badly for his behaviour. He noted that while he didn't approve of fighting outside the octagon, he could make an exception on this occasion as he would do the same thing to anyone who dares to provoke his motherland. In essence, it was all brought back down to the political context at every turn, symbolic propaganda via the most cheesy rhetoric.

This caused others to capitulate quickly, too.

Khabib has travelled the world, all too willing to meet any Muslim leader who wants him for an opportunistic, populist photoshoot. Ramzan Kadyrov made him an honorary citizen of Chechnya. There's been Crown Prince Hussein of Jordan; a back and forth with Hamad bin Isa Al Khalifa of Bahrain; Recep Erdoğan got in on the act in Turkey; and recently, he was even in Saudi Arabia. There, Mohammed bin Salman might not have met with him in person, but the invitation had been extended by one of the many foundations owned by the country's de facto ruler.

They say imitation is the highest form of flattery.

Thus McGregor ought to be flattered, but is this really a method to follow given where it has gotten him so fast and furiously? Granted, they are at different points of the roller coaster.

Recently, there's been a feeling that the Notorious has lost not just the fear of defeat but the care for fighting, and that his self-worth was tied up in body parts that have started to betray him. He may get in the octagon again — and people will watch — but the magic has left the building. It's like a kid at Disneyland who catches a glimpse of Mickey Mouse on break, his head off, smoking a fag and sipping from a hip flask.

Back at the parade, it'll never be the same.

'Breaking news …'

In Dublin, the radio goes on. As details emerge, there is still a large degree of whom to believe around it. Ahmed Abdirzak, a 22-year-old from London, says McGregor didn't object to the photo, but as he made his way towards him, he had put out his hand to say hello. Yet

McGregor grabbed his arm, held it tight so he couldn't get away, and went berserk from there. At around 5.20am, he was finally arrested at a beachfront mansion located less than five miles from the incident. While McGregor's behaviour on this occasion was relatively minor against his own past, the state of Florida doesn't care.

He's back, walking a tightrope and hoping for the best. Where once his discipline put so much in his hands, now his ego has seen him leave his future in the hands of others.

In July 2018, he negotiated a plea deal in New York that crucially avoided a felony charge. It was crucial, because as a foreign national, such a charge would have had consequences for both his career and his future. After all, conviction for a violent felony can lead the Department of Homeland Security to seek deportation of a non-citizen or render them inadmissible for future re-entry. That would be a blow for him, because Americans love a redemption story, often forcing that artificial narrative when it's not really there. But if not present, he wouldn't have that opportunity: he would have been confined to the same small quarters he grew up in and to the same influences that have pulled him back down to this point.

When we met in 2013, there's no doubt there was mischief. He was like the giddy kid in class who was supposed to stay quiet, but when they spoke up it was actually quite funny and never out of badness. Those influences have seen him change, however. Now, he's like the deranged kid throwing a book at the teacher's head out of hate.

They say every problem is an opportunity in disguise, but for McGregor, the opportunity has become the problem. It's why those around Irish MMA have slowly distanced themselves from him. It's why John Kavanagh makes sure he treads softly, softly, so he can disassociate himself from any horrific moments that may occur in the future. It's why even national broadcaster RTÉ's showing of McGregor's documentary over Christmas felt less like an inspirational story being sold to the nation's youth and more like the sanitised promotion of a dangerous lie being skipped over because of fame and fortune.

It all has the feel of a ticking clock, of walking on river ice in spring.

There are eventually some form of consequences, even if someone appears to get away with all their wrongs.

A working-class hero was something to be.

* * *

APRIL IN IRELAND COMES AROUND.

Days stretch.

Flowers threaten.

Summer promises.

It's six months now since McGregor was beaten. His reaction?

The leaky drip of breaking news has become a flooding torrent.

He announces his retirement from the UFC. A person close to the situation sends me a WhatsApp within minutes, rubbishing another publicity stunt performed to keep himself relevant. 'I don't think he's genuine about anything anymore,' it reads. 'If I was to speculate, WrestleMania, cause a stir, back in the octagon before the end of the year.'

He's right about the stir, but it doesn't happen via WWE.

The idea of a rematch has been put on the stove and begins to bubble. McGregor posts a photo of Khabib's wedding on social media, his wife's head covered in traditional dress. And then he goes full xenophobic. 'Your wife is a towel mate.'

Dana White condemns it. The circle is almost complete again.

Khabib is different this time though. The mimic. Aiming low. He posts a photo of McGregor with the woman in Liverpool claiming to have had his child, captioned, 'Rapist, you are rapist [sic]. You are a hypocrite who is not responsible for your actions. Justice will find you. We will see.'

Dana White condemns it.

This is surely bedrock.

But perhaps the biggest of all breaking news isn't really news at all. An internationally renowned news organisation domiciled in the USA have decided to publish the serious criminal allegations about McGregor. The news is online, easily available at the click of a mouse to anyone in Ireland or beyond. But no Irish news outlet is able to repeat or even signpost the allegations under the terms of the Criminal Law Act 1981. Commonality under EU law also prevents publications and news organisations in Europe from doing so too.

The allegations were unproven, and the existence of an investigation did not imply that McGregor was guilty of a crime. When I contacted McGregor's representatives about the allegations I received no response. After taking legal advice the best I can do is to quote a redacted version of the story. It says more about the absurdity of the law in Ireland than it does about McGregor.

'*Conor McGregor, the Ultimate Fighting Championship's biggest star and one of the world's highest-paid athletes, is under investigation in Ireland* ███████████████████████ *according to four people familiar with the investigation. McGregor has not been charged with a crime.* ████████████████

████████████████████████████████████

████████████████████████████████████

████████████████████████████████████

████████████ *The allegations have not been proved, and the fact that an investigation is continuing does not imply that McGregor is guilty of a crime. A lawyer for McGregor in Dublin did not respond to messages seeking comment.*

████████████████████████████████████

████████████████████████████████████

████████████████████████████████████

The Irish news media have reported on the case since ████████████████████ *late last year, but without naming McGregor. Laws in Ireland restrict the news media from identifying individuals charged with* ██ *unless they are convicted, which has not happened in this case.*

'A spokesman for Ireland's police service, known as the Garda, would not confirm if McGregor is the suspect. ████████████

McGregor and the UFC have not commented on the allegations.'

Enough.

I walk into a pub in central Dublin in the hope that a few beers will take the edges off this idea of a troubled sports star who had so much going for him not so long ago, copying a world that had so much going for it not so long ago. Here, though, memories of that dive bar in Vegas come rushing back for a myriad of reasons. It's not so much the man with his haggard face and the dirty, matted hair of someone with a past well worth hearing about. It's not so much the sharp, acidic aftershave that first grabbed hold of a sense and caused a twist of the head before sight quickly took over. It's definitely not the mix of prostitutes who'd been driven away from the high rollers and fancier digs by the new and fresh desperation of those with youth on their side, and a sad and sordid sort who wished they could afford them for just an hour of less loneliness. It's obviously not the tales of Mexican cartels and art galleries, of forthcoming books and upcoming films, of far-away sea and sand and sex in Brazil.

But scratch at the surface and, listening in, maybe here and there aren't so different.

Stateside, it's a similar conversation but turned up louder. In Dublin there are the same ills sweeping across the landscape like a plague. To the right of me, a guy starts up a topic about an immigrant family down the road. It's vicious. It's nasty. It's bullshit. And still, there's agreement rather than someone standing up against it. This is the populism that comes about from a financial crash rather than a recession. It's not even about the idea of there being less money but rather the fact that the inequality between wallets has been so big for so long. The driving notion becomes that 'someone' took these people's things and that they are going to get them back.

It provides a political and business opportunity by exploiting fear and ignorance.

It would be easy to interject in the conversation, but what's the point? When you are raised by wolves, you crawl on all fours. It's just that scenario playing out over drink.

McGregor comes to mind as they babble on.

Did he come from this? Did he escape from this?

Was it his making? Will it be his downfall?

That's to be decided, but if he has peaked as an athlete, what about the rest of his life? They say nothing sharpens the mind like standing at the very edge of a precipice. Not all see it coming, though, walking clean off the ledge none the wiser until the sudden drop.

Sometimes, as well as hate, you also get words of wisdom in such places as this Dublin watering hole. People who have sat and listened and contemplated rather than stood and talked and argued. To the left of me, an older man starts up a conversation, and I tell him about this book. He pauses.

Finally, he asks, 'You know on the headstone, the two numbers that indicate when you were born and when you died?'

'Sure.'

'Well, did you ever look at the dash in between them?'

'I can't say I really have.'

'Think about it. That little dash is your whole life. So what has Conor McGregor done with his dash?'

It's a fascinating concept. It is one that requires much more thought.

Ultimately, we agree that it comes back to a sense of legacy, because otherwise, what's the point of all this? And maybe McGregor's hasn't been defined yet. Maybe great things await, and maybe one day he'll look back with some shame on elements of the story so far and be a new man. With the pages of this one running out, that's another chapter for another time.

However, as much as Conor McGregor pretends, this is not Hollywood. It's Dublin.

And where he comes from, there tends not to be a happy ending.

After all, people don't always know what they've become until it's too late.

ACKNOWLEDGMENTS

TO MAKE THIS HAPPEN, A LOT OF PEOPLE WERE KIND
enough to give their time and thoughts.

And closer to home, their patience.

First off thanks to my wife Erika. I can be grumpy enough at the best of times, but writing a book takes it to a new level, and her tolerance and support throughout the process meant an awful lot and that this was actually possible. I'd also like to thank my dog Putchi as those long evening walks were often the peace and quiet needed after long days. On top of that thanks to my family back home in Ireland who have always stood by me and those in Brazil who adopted me.

To Wright Thompson who was kind enough to write the foreword to this. Having you on board meant a huge amount as I've long been a massive admirer of your work.

To James Corbett for his support and endless work in putting this together and to all those at deCoubertin Books who had to endure draft after draft, and made this a far better read.

To Gavan Casey and Joe Callaghan for their company on days and nights in Vegas, the sort that could break a man but instead provided memories worth holding onto.

To John Byrne for yet one more dig out during the Dublin element of this, your kindness won't be forgotten. And to Karol Dillon, Louise Caraher and Tony Flynn who have always been great sounding boards for articles in other spheres, and were again for this.

To Orin Starn, William Todd Schultz, Mark Bauerlein and David Marshall for their academic insight into a changing and collapsing society riddled with celebrity culture. As someone who didn't make it through university, I was naturally in awe but this experience only added to that.

Thanks to Kurt Badenhausen for opening up the books on the financials behind both McGregor and the UFC. To Stitch Duran for breaking bread and filling me in on his remarkable experiences with all the humility of a man that didn't forget where he came from. To Karim Zidan whose work around MMA and society continues to fascinate. To Kenneth Egan whose friendship also began with a book many years ago and never wilted. To Floyd Landis who remains one of the most fascinating people in sport, and whose mind has even surpassed his cycling exploits.

Thanks to the brilliant and brave Nicola Tallant, and to Mark O'Toole, Ken Early, Donald McRae and Paul Kimmage for their knowledge and great direction. Thanks to John Kavanagh – we may have started out on the wrong foot but that's part of the fun. Thanks to Paschal Collins for keeping it real when so many who did as much didn't.

To fighting men like Paulie Malignaggi, Dave Hill and Artemij Sitenkov who aided with their insight from inside the gym and inside the ring. To Phil Sutcliffe and Stephen Kavanagh, who are the real cornerstones of sport despite the lack of recognition.

To the man at the bar in Las Vegas, may the girl in Brazil be real. To the man at the bar in Drimnagh, may the winter pass, the heart continue to hold up, and the batteries work.

Most of all though to Conor McGregor, who has lived this life. I can but hope these allegations are false, and that your story is far from finished. If so, may the destination serve you well and may the journey teach you much.

www.decoubertin.co.uk